Pearl

ANNE RUCK

AN OMF BOOK

Copyright © Overseas Missionary Fellowship
(formerly China Inland Mission)

First published *1986*

ISBN 9971-972-37-9

OMF BOOKS are distributed by
OMF, 404 South Church Street,
Robesonia, Pa, 19551, USA;
OMF, Belmont, The Vine,
Sevenoaks, Kent, TN13 3TZ;
OMF, PO Box 177, Kew East,
Victoria 3102, Australia,
and other OMF offices.

Published by Overseas Missionary Fellowship (IHQ) Ltd,
2 Cluny Road, Singapore 1025, Republic of Singapore.

Printed by Kyodo-Shing Loong Printing Industries Pte Ltd

CONTENTS

Chapter One	1
Chapter Two	8
Chapter Three	16
Chapter Four	27
Chapter Five	32
Chapter Six	39
Chapter Seven	44
Chapter Eight	55
Chapter Nine	62
Chapter Ten	71
Chapter Eleven	79
Chapter Twelve	91
Chapter Thirteen	95
Chapter Fourteen	105
Chapter Fifteen	112
Chapter Sixteen	119
Chapter Seventeen	128
Chapter Eighteen	140
Chapter Nineteen	150
Postscript	158

CHAPTER ONE

The chickens squawked and scattered as Beni's red Honda skidded to a halt on the sandy soil. Mutiara slipped down from the back, where she had been perching sidesaddle, her school books on her knee.

"Are you coming in for a minute?"

"Well," Beni glanced at his watch, then reached down to lock the machine. "Just a minute then. I really must get back early today."

And every day. Mutiara smiled bleakly as she crossed the short plank over the ditch and pushed back the bolt on the wooden gate. A group of children were playing marbles on the hard, well-swept earth under the banana tree. They barely glanced up as she walked by, and neither did the scraggy dog which lay dozing, head on paws, by the doorstep. Mutiara paused in the doorway to ease off her shoes and to wait for Beni. His shirt and trousers gleamed crisply white, even after a long, sweat-sticky day; his keys jangled, sparkling, in his hand as he strolled up the path.

"Come on, then!" He gave her a gentle shove and followed her into the house. "Don't just stand there daydreaming!" He had kept his shoes on, dark, well-polished leather slip-ons.

People sometimes did and sometimes did not remove their shoes when entering a house; Mutiara felt it each time as a comment on Beni's attitude to her home. But then Mutiara considered, and weighed, and analyzed, and strove to interpret, just about everything that Beni did or said.

The long, sparsely-furnished room seemed dark after the glare of the tropical sun outside. Patchy grey-green walls, black polished floor, red plastic-leather settee and armchairs arranged geometrically, in two precise rectangles, each around its glass-topped coffee table. The Lord Jesus talked with some disciples on a huge calendar by the window, while across the room an airline poster showed misty girls rambling through a tea plantation. Four brown doors spaced at intervals along one wall added to the gloom and the feeling of being in a long corridor or waiting room.

But at the far end the drab neatness erupted into chaos. A small table stood against the wall, piled high with textbooks which were propped open at a dozen different angles. More books and papers rose haphazardly from nearby chairs, and lined the top of the television. A row of five glasses, thick coffee-sludged at the bottom, stood to attention behind a blank notepad on the table. On the floor were strewn about twenty scrumpled balls of paper. Mesmerized on the chair, with his back to them as they came in, sat David, Mutiara's elder by two years and a student at the University of North Sumatra.

"Hi there, Genius! What's the great Professor doing today, then?" Beni lifted three files from the settee and dropped them carefully on the floor before sitting down heavily. "They work you hard enough, don't they? Or is this all for show? I thought a student's life was supposed to be carefree!"

"Hello, Beni. I might just as well have been out enjoying myself for all I've achieved in the last two hours. Saturation point, I suppose."

David took careful aim and shot his next ball of paper into a vase on the low table. "Are you fixing some drinks then, Tara? Something long and cool would be great — I'm up to here with caffeine."

"Seriously though," said Beni as he stretched out his legs and cracked his finger joints. "What's wrong with that engineering faculty? Sweated labour, is it? All you engineers seem to do nothing but work."

David retrieved one of his rejects from the floor and carefully smoothed out the paper, scanning the row of figures absentmindedly before discarding it again. He look up with solemn eyes.

"I've got to work, Beni," he said, "The registration money to get me into university just about crippled Dad, let alone the tuition fees and everything else on top. I can't let it all be wasted. I feel I've got to work hard now to make it worth while." He gazed round at the finger-smeared wall and the telltale damp patches on the ceiling. "And

I've got to, *got* to get a good job at the end of it all."

"Yes, yes, of course, the dutiful son and all that. Very good, I'm sure. Only don't take it too far — you've got to live a little too, you know, before you die." Beni yawned as he flicked the pages of a science magazine. He himself would be going to Jakarta next year, to one of the top universities in Indonesia. He had no worries about the entrance money. The contract on one of his father's houses expired soon, and a new three year lease, payable in advance, would cover all his needs. Passing the exam would be easy too, he was sure, thanks to his father's contacts in administration. He was looking forward to the freedom of living away from home. Not that his parents interfered much in what he did — they were rarely home themselves to see. If only they would let him change the Honda for a new Jimney jeep — a slick white one with black upholstery and a powerful cassette player. Beni knew little, and cared less, of the stresses facing less well-endowed families.

"English too," he added, impressed, his eyes flitting across the open textbooks. "Isn't it time some of these were translated into Indonesian? Do they expect you to be a linguist as well as an engineer?"

"It isn't easy," David admitted. "That's what takes half the time, in fact. But more are being translated all the time. And at least the technical words are the same."

"Well, *I* think you need a break. Don't you think so, lovely?" Beni's fingers played a tune on Mutiara's arm as she put the tray of drinks on the low table. "He needs a break, doesn't he now?" Taking hold of her hand, Beni pulled her gently down beside him on the settee. She leaned back, enjoying his casual air of ownership, and the sense of "we two", as a couple, discussing David's problem. She sipped her passion fruit juice in a haze. *Surely,* she thought, *we belong together like this. It's so right, somehow.*

"Give it a rest tonight, Dave. You want to sweep this lot right away and forget all about it." Beni was still talking to her brother. "You're coming to Youth Group, aren't you?"

"Oh, I don't know. I'll think about it. It's this assignment, you see."

"Assignment nothing, David. We need you. They want the group to do a spot in the service on Sunday, and this is the one chance we'll get to practise. Bring your guitar along, right? Oh, and don't forget to bring Tara!" He smiled at her, that special you-and-me-together smile, tossed back his drink and stood up, all in one graceful but decided movement.

"Must go, Ra." He caught up his keys, and in a couple of smooth strides was at the door. "Make a quick getaway before your Ma comes out and grabs me!" Beni laughed, but Mutiara wondered, not for the first time, why he always seemed to be avoiding her parents.

"You won't stay ..." she hesitated, "Have something to eat here ... then we could all go together?"

"Uh huh," Beni shook his head. "Have to call somewhere first."

He was already striding down the path, and she trailed after him, searching her mind for delaying topics to keep him talking at the gate. But he was out, and astride the motor bike, before she knew it.

"Thanks for bringing me home. I wish you could've stayed a bit longer."

"Keep smiling, Tara! Make him come, won't you — we can't sing without a bass guitar. See you!"

A flick of the switch and he was off, the Honda jerking forward like a warhorse into battle. Mutiara stood watching as he skimmed over stones and skirted round potholes, swaying from one side of the road to the other and stirring a cloud of dust in his wake. It was twilight, that dusky half hour before the sudden blackness that descends so finally in the tropics. The red and white of motor cycle and rider merged into other colours; green hedge, brown hens, a mottled browny purple splodge of children playing; a green and yellow *becak*[1], the driver pedalling slowly and heavily while on the passenger seat a fat woman hunched her shoulders over a bulging shopping bag. The

---

[1] Trishaw.

hypnotic flare of a hissing hurricane lamp came gradually closer and formed itself into a handcart selling noodle soup.

Make him come, won't you. And if he doesn't come, how can I go? There had been no mention of Beni calling round to collect her. *What do you really think, my darling Beni?*

"Yes, he's a bit smooth, but he's all right really."

She started. "Dave! You made me jump! You shouldn't come creeping up on people like that!"

"But I've been here all the time, Tara. We walked down the path together, remember? I was here when you said goodbye to Beni."

"No you weren't!" Uncertainty and a sort of horror — what might she have said? Then doubtfully, "Were you really there, David? You're not having me on? I never even saw you!"

"I was right beside you, Tara. You must be in love!" David laughed. "No eyes for anyone but Beni! ... I've heard them say that love is blind, but this is ... Hey, wait a minute, there's no need to get upset — I'm only joking!"

Mutiara was standing rigid, her hands to her head and a look of dismay, almost of fear, in her eyes. "No .. no .. it's just that ... Oh, what's *wrong* with me?"

Before he could answer she had fled inside.

David walked slowly up the path feeling concerned. Tara was clearly getting herself into a state about something, and he suspected there was more to it than the usual boyfriend-girlfriend affair.

CHAPTER TWO

The dark kitchen was smoky, and the mixture of kerosene flames, hot oil, chillies and garlic caught at Mutiara's throat and made her cough. Elvira, next sister down, stood poised with a handful of green leaves which she tossed into the wok and pushed quickly from side to side.

"Superman gone home, then?" she asked as she stirred the *sawi*[1] to and fro with a brisk, jerky movement. "I don't know why he bothers to come in. Never stays very long, does he, these days?"

"He's busy at the moment. Got a lot of things on." Mutiara lifted the heavy rice cooker carefully off the stove and began ladling the rice into a large bowl. "It takes him quite far enough out of his way just bringing me home from school every day."

"What's he busy *doing*, though?"

"Oh Vira, just leave it, can't you! Don't keep on so!"

Mutiara banged the bowl down on the table and went out to summon the younger children. She found them mending a toy with David on the back porch.

---

[1] Green leafy vegetable.

"What about tonight, then?" he asked her. "Do you want me to take you to Youth Group?"

"That would be nice, David. Yes please." She smiled at him gratefully. "If you're sure you don't mind being dragged away from your work. We could skip the Bible study and go along a bit later, if you like?"

"Naughty!"

As it happened, the discussion was already in full swing by the time David and Mutiara arrived at the church hall.

"What about a motor bike? Can I ask God for a motor bike?"

"Make it a big one!"

"It depends what you want it for." Yesaya, chairman of the youth group, who was leading the meeting, looked thoughtful. "If it's only for selfish reasons, no go. But if you want to use it to serve God, go ahead and ask — *expecting* God to provide it!"

"Come on in, you two," said the missionary, James Stephens, seeing them in the doorway. "Glad you could make it. We're talking about faith. What it means in practice."

The others edged round to make room for them. Mutiara slipped shyly into the nearest seat, looking round with an anxious crease between her brows; then flushed and smiled as she caught Beni's eye across the room. He was sitting next to Rita, who sang in the group. Tara disliked her intensely.

"What are you praying for, Tara?" asked the other in a low, silky voice. "Or don't we need to ask?" She shifted her chair, quite unnecessarily Tara thought, until she was almost on top of Beni.

"This meeting I was at," Yesaya was explaining, "The preacher said that Abraham had faith, right? We all know that. But did you realize how *rich* Abraham was? Did you know he was one of the wealthiest men around. Kind of big businessman, only in his case it was stockbreeding. Think about it — all the cattle and sheep he had. The Bible said God had blessed Abraham in all things — and that includes financially too." He looked round the circle to make sure they were all following. "And *we*, you and me, are the children of Abraham, the heirs of Abraham, this preacher said, if only we have the faith to believe it. So we can ask God to make us wealthy too — just like Abraham!"

Yesaya had the clear but rugged good looks that television advertisers are so fond of; tall, dark of course, with strong shoulders yet an air of control, of self-containment, which came perhaps from his karate training. He had had quite a reputation in the university as a karate champion, and the aura remained, even though he had given up karate, very suddenly, a year or so back. Now his energies were directed along strictly Christian lines. He was eager to stretch himself spiritually, eager to grow and to learn, from whatever quarter, eager to share what he was learning.

"So what do you think, then? Shoot me down, if you like." He leaned back, arms folded.

"We can *ask*, Yesaya, sure," drawled Beni, "And God can say No, can't he?"

"Oh no, that's not faith," said Yesaya, exasperated. "Not this Yes, No, Wait thing. That's not believing God answers prayer. That's excuses for not getting answers." He sighed. "I'm talking about faith now, F-A-I-T-H. Do you believe that God can do miracles? Like ... like ..."

"My brother had a funny experience," put in one of the other boys. "He was on this business trip to the Philippines, see, and they have all this television over there, see, ever so many channels. He was watching this TV pastor, and he says, 'Want to give up smoking?' The pastor, that is, the pastor says it, and he says, 'Anyone has trouble giving up smoking, you ring this number and I'll pray for you to give it up.' Really! So that's what he did; my brother I mean, he rang up the pastor, and he hasn't smoked since!"

"No!"

"Don't believe you!"

"It's true! If ever he gets the urge to light up a cigarette, he thinks about this pastor praying for him in the Philippines, and somehow he doesn't want to smoke any more."

"What do you think about smoking, Pak[2] James? Should a Christian smoke?" Beni knocked the ash off his cigarette and looked meaningfully at the English minister, who did not smoke.

Jim thought of the acrid, throat-catching, eye-smarting, smoke-laden atmosphere that accompanied most major decision-making meetings in the church.

"I think we're getting away from the subject a bit," he said.

"Do you want to add your comments on faith, before we close the discussion?" asked Yesaya.

"Yes, thank you." He paused, wondering what to say. He wanted to encourage Yesaya, and yet ... "I think it's been very helpful to think through the nature of Abraham's faith together. He believed God, didn't he, against all the odds — Sarah's age and so on. And his faith meant commitment; he had to leave home and go off into the unknown. And it meant obedience; he had to be ready to sacrifice Isaac. And that's the context in which God blessed him so richly. We need to remember that. And I think we do have to ask ourselves, is our faith sometimes too small."

"And the answer is, yes it is too small, but let's hope what we've learned tonight will increase it a bit," said Yesaya. "We'll close in prayer now, and then the group have to practise for Sunday."

They practised in the shadowy church, Mutiara

---

[2]Short for *Bapak* — literally "father", used for "Mr."

CHAPTER TWO

turning the pages for Yesaya at the organ. David played bass guitar to Beni's treble. Rita sang beautifully, as Tara reluctantly admitted to herself.

"We need another girl, really," said Beni, "To balance the voices better. Come on, Tara love, you'll sing too, won't you?"

"No, don't ask her," laughed Rita. "Poor Tara, she never could hold a tune, could you? There's no point in embarrassing the poor girl."

Mutiara bit her lip hard to keep away the tears.

"Now let's try this one more time," put in Yesaya. "Remember not to rush that last part. You're supposed to be working with me, remember, not racing to see who can finish first."

The missionary came in as they were singing the last verse.

"That girl has a lovely voice, doesn't she?" he murmured to Mutiara. She wished she had stayed at home.

"Who wants a lift?" asked Jim when they finally packed up. Yesaya, David and Mutiara gratefully accepted. Rita, it seemed, would go on Beni's Honda, as she lived on his side of town.

"That girl gives me a headache," muttered Mutiara to David as they bounced along in the back of the jeep. "And I mean a real physical one!"

"Oh don't be silly, Tara. You're just a whole lot too possessive about Beni. You don't own him. And it's natural he should take Rita home when he practically has to drive by her door."

"No, really," said Mutiara. "I do have a

headache, just here above my eye ... Well, it's more *in* my eye, come to think of it."

Yesaya was still talking about Abraham in the front. Mutiara thought a bit, looked at her brother, then down at her feet. "She doesn't like me, you know, Rita doesn't. She's had her eye on Beni since before ever he and I got together." Mutiara spoke quietly but with conviction. "She's been playing the spirits, Dave, I'm sure of it."

David looked at her blankly. "Playing the spirits? What do you mean?"

"I mean I think she's been to the *dukun*[3]. She's been using some medicine or charm or something. There's plenty of girls do that, you know ... get a medicine from the *dukun*, a potion, when they want to steal someone else's boyfriend. Only this time it's not a love mix." She paused. "That's what's so hard to take, Dave, it's not just to make Beni love her. She's *hurting* me — and she's doing something that makes it so I can't see properly!"

David stared at his sister in consternation. Whatever was the matter with her?

"Tara, are you mad? Rita is a Christian! She's not buying love potions or anything else! Of course she likes Beni, lots of girls do, but it's still you he brings home from school every day and takes to parties and things. No one's putting a spell on him — or you either!"

---

[3] A man who heals people using local medicines, usually through evil spirits.

"But you don't understand, David! Something's happening to me — something strange. Like this afternoon when I didn't see you standing right by me." The sudden glare from another car's headlights showed Mutiara's face distressed and anxious.

"Tara, don't worry so!" said David. "If you think something's wrong with you, why not go to the doctor? It's probably something quite simple that can be dealt with in no time by taking a few drops or having your eyes tested or something. Don't let yourself get into a state and start imagining things." He smiled reassuringly. "You'll be all right, Tara, honestly!"

"All right, I'll see a doctor." Mutiara nodded in the darkness and gave a wobbly smile. She did not feel, somehow, that it was a simple thing. There was something wrong, really wrong, but it was not yet quite definite enough for her to put her finger on what it was.

CHAPTER THREE

Mutiara did not go to the doctor, however, until much later; a mistake which she was to regret.

In the cold morning light her fears had seemed insubstantial; the fancies of a jealous imagination.

"It's not as if I were going blind," she explained to her mother, "Or seeing spots before the eyes! It's just that ... well ... " she paused. "Say I'm looking down here, chopping up these onions. Then I don't seem to see you standing over there in the doorway."

Ibu[1] Sitompul looked puzzled. "But you wouldn't do, would you? If I'm looking at one thing I don't expect to be seeing something else that's in a different place entirely."

"No, I know you don't. But all the same you do see it, in a way, sort of round the side, somehow."

"Do I?" asked her mother doubtfully.

"*You* do — but *I* don't."

"She wants eyes in the back of her head," called Elvira from the bathroom where she was scrubbing the clothes. "Which you need when your boyfriend's playing around!"

---

[1] Mrs. (lit.: Mother)

"Beni is *not* playing around, Vira! I don't know why you're always getting at him!"

"I never mentioned Beni! Did I, mum?"

"I think you've been studying too hard," said their mother, "Straining your eyes with all that reading. Perhaps you need glasses."

"Tell you what — you can try mine, Tara. I never wear them and they'd suit you." Elvira wiped the soap off her hands and ran off to look for her glasses.

"It's a pity you're on afternoon school this year," mused Ibu Sitompul. "You don't get home till turned six, and that's too late to be going to the doctor. But I think Dr. Hutabarat has an early morning surgery at her home, about eightish. We could go round there tomorrow morning, if you like, just for a check up — leave the cooking till later?"

"No Mum, it's a waste of time, honestly." If her mother was unconvinced it seemed unlikely that a doctor would understand such vague symptoms. "She'd only take my blood pressure and give me a vitamin injection, like they always do. And there's Rp.3,000 gone for nothing. I'd be better stopping off at the chemist's, for some eyedrops."

"Look, here they are!" Elvira came in triumphantly with the glasses. "Do try them, Tara. I specially chose blue tinted lenses, but then I never wear blue. It's ages since I've used them."

Mutiara rubbed the glasses on a cloth and tried them on, rather gingerly, then blinked a few times.

"Yes, it does seem a bit clearer, brighter ... But it's too dark in this kitchen!" She went out into the yard and looked slowly round, at the hens, the mango tree, the broken bicycle against the wall. "It's closer, a bit sharper, maybe ... But it's all crowding in on me!" She put out a hand, as if to touch the tree, but it was too far away. "I might bump into things ... Where's a mirror?"

Elvira followed her into the bedroom.

"Yes, they make you look good, Tara — more sophisticated. They never looked anything on me. I hate them."

"It's kind of you, Vira. I'll try them for a day or two, anyway." Mutiara smiled at her sister, who shrugged offhandedly and turned away.

Mutiara lingered in front of the mirror, examining her face and wondering what Beni thought of girls in glasses. *They're not bad at all. But everything looks so weird through these lenses — makes my head swim. I'll be dizzy. And really, wearing glasses won't help my problem.* She sighed. Perhaps eyedrops would do the trick.

Beni found her in a corner of the classroom on Saturday afternoon, squinting up at the ceiling with her head well back, while a friend squeezed some drops into each eye.

"What's up, Ra? I've been looking all over for you! You sick or something?"

"Oh hello, Beni." Mutiara pulled herself upright and pushed her hair back over her shoulders. "I've been having trouble with my eyesight, so I've started putting these drops in." She picked up the little bottle and held it out. "New Life for Tired Eyes, it says."

"Well, they give you a nice sparkle, Big Eyes," said Beni, "Better than those antique specs you've been wearing lately."

Mutiara's friend frowned at him, and walked out of the room.

"Thanks a lot, Ani!" Mutiara called out after her.

Beni perched on a desk and swung his legs. "The thing is, Ra, that I can't take you home today."

"Oh."

"My cousin's here, and we've got to go trailing over to the other side of Medan to fix something up."

"Oh."

"But it's all right for tonight, isn't it? You still want to see that film?" She nodded. "The thing is," Beni looked awkward for a moment. "Well — I'm not sure how long this is going to take. So it looks like I'd better meet you there. Is that all right?"

Mutiara nodded again, more slowly. Her parents were so particular; they liked a date to come to the house and make stilted conversation for a few minutes so that they could weigh him up and lay down rules about not being out too late. They liked everything to be proper and "official". So did she. But they did know Beni; they approved of her having a boyfriend from such a "good family". And really, it was time they moved up into the nineteen eighties a bit!

"Tell you what," said Beni, not entirely understanding her hesitation, "It's at the Medan Plaza, isn't it? Fourth floor, right? You go to the third floor, have a look round the supermarket, and I'll join you there. Then if I'm held up you won't just be hanging around." He did a quick calculation on his fingers. "If you get there a little bit after seven — say I'm through quickly, then we've time for a beefburger first. If I'm longer over Teladan way then we see the film first and eat later. Right?"

"Right," said Mutiara.

He stood up and bent to brush the chalk off his trousers. "If I'm not there by eight then go straight up and I'll meet you at the ticket office. See you!" He squeezed her shoulder and was gone.

The Medan Plaza was a new modern shopping complex, complete with escalators, bright lights, and blaring music. The first two floors were mostly shops; on the third, besides the Metro supermarket and department store, was an array of eating places, from Hasty Hooston fried chicken to Javanese *soto ayam*[2] and on to ice cream. The cinema was on the floor above, and right at the top was a children's fairground. On Saturday nights the whole place was a seething mass of people; girlfriends and boyfriends, mothers and children,

---

[2] Chicken soup cooked in coconut milk

aunts and uncles and cousins; playing, viewing, eating, strolling, scrutinizing, comparing prices, bargaining, and occasionally buying.

Ani had agreed to come along with Mutiara and her sister Elvira decided to join them. They sauntered down the row of shoe shops; at each one Ani tried on shoes, stood up, sat down, turned this way and that, haggled a little over prices and then left. Finally they went back to the first shop, and she bought a pair of red shoes with high heels at a slightly higher price than she had hoped for. Next they headed for a cassette stall, and perched on swivel stools listening to different groups until a gang of boys drifted in and stood leaning over them making funny comments. They went up a couple of floors then, to the supermarket, and walked slowly up and down, up and down the aisles; china and glass, plastic containers, stationery, toys, hairdryers, hairsprays and toothpaste, dried fish, cans of Western food, fizzy drinks, and back to the chinaware.

"It's nearly eight o'clock," said Elvira, "But where oh where is our Superman?" She stood on tiptoes, peering over the heads of the slowly moving crowd. "Did we miss him in the toy section? Who's that there playing with an army jeep?"

Ani kicked her. "I think Beni must have got held up in the traffic," she said. "Do you want to walk round again?"

"Well," Tara looked doubtful.

"Better go on up," said Elvira. "Just in case he shows. Got to wait in line till he finishes his first engagement of the evening."

"Shut up, Vira." Ani took Tara's arm and led her out through the check-out. "We'll get something to eat at one of the stalls here. You go and wait by the ticket office as arranged." She pushed Tara towards the escalator. "If Beni's really late you can always come back and join us till he comes."

"Thanks Ani," said Tara. "He might have got caught in a *razzia*[3] or something."

She stepped on to the escalator, and the other two girls went over to the nearest stall and ordered a chicken rice each, choosing a table with an easy view of the escalators.

Near the entrance to the cinema was a huge goldfish tank, aglow with a myriad of tiny red, gold and black fishes, darting hither and thither, ever moving, ever searching, in the silent water. The single fluorescent light above the tank created a warm circle in the dim alcove. Mutiara stood watching the flashes of colour. She had not allowed herself to wonder just where Beni had been going, or who his relative was. "Cousin" could mean anything — even the sex was unclear in a language with unisex pronouns.

Three boys with fifties hairstyles were lounging against the ticket office counter; the same ones

---
[3]Police road-check

who had been in the cassette shop earlier. One in particular, the tallest, kept looking her up and down in a way which made her flesh crawl. Eventually he detached himself from the group and wandered over.

"Want to see the film, then?" he asked. "Where's your friends?"

Mutiara looked at the fish and said nothing.

"How about we team up, then?" He smiled and nudged her. "Three and three ... That's about right, isn't it?" he added with a wink.

Mutiara gazed at the darting fishes.

"Come on, then! I'm asking you! Back row, yes?" He made to take her arm and she pushed him away, pulse racing. "Conceited, is it?"

The other boys made as if to join them. Tara did not wait to see. She marched briskly to the top of the escalator, passing within a couple of metres of Beni, who was walking slowly towards her with his arms outstretched and a rueful smile on his face. His smile turned to a look of astonishment as she strode by him, eyes blazing, and stepped on to the moving escalator.

"Tara," he started, but she was already moving downwards out of sight. He raced to the bannister and leaned over. "Say, Tara ... Well ... Ach!" he exclaimed angrily. You might at least let me say I'm sorry!" He looked at his watch. "It's only ten past eight!"

Mutiara did not join the family at church the next

morning. She stayed in bed with a headache and a sick stomach. And in fact, she did feel quite sick at the thought of last night.

"Had a row with Beni," Elvira told David in a thrilled whisper. "We saw it all, Ani and I. They were going to a film together and Beni was late. He goes bounding up the escalator — and two seconds later she comes bounding down — practically falling over herself. Just ignores us, sitting with our chicken rice — stands like an idiot staring into space until Ani goes and more or less leads her by the hand."

"Really?" David remembered the silent way Tara had come in last night and gone straight to bed.

"Beni didn't come down though. We must have sat there half an hour — Tara not saying a word and Ani chattering away about nothing. Nobody mentions Beni, of course. I suppose he decided to go and see the film by himself ... I was all for going to see it ourselves, but Ani kept giving me those kill-you-at-twenty-paces looks, every time I tried to suggest it. Anyway, we'd have missed half of it — and you never catch up on the story, do you?"

David decided he would have a word with Beni after the service.

It was late that evening before he had a chance to talk to Mutiara about it. He found her on the back porch, leaning back with her eyes shut in a broken old rattan chair.

"Is something up between you and Beni?" he

asked, going straight to the point. It took a few minutes for Tara to answer.

"We were supposed to be going to a film together last night ... but he never came." Her eyes were still tightly closed.

"He wasn't all that late, though, was he? Ten minutes he said — and that was mostly looking for a parking place. He'd borrowed his father's car to do you in style."

Mutiara pulled a piece of rattan out from somewhere under the chair seat, and began twisting it this way and that in her hands.

"And then you brushed straight past him without even letting him say a word!"

"I was so humiliated," said Tara softly, her fingers working the rattan and her eyes still closed. "There were these awful boys making up to me and I just couldn't stay there a moment longer. I had to get away ... " Gradually she became aware of what David had said. "Brushed past him? ... I went before he came, Dave. I know I should have waited ... oh yes I *would* have waited, if it wasn't for those boys just staring at me ... I kept thinking, Beni, why don't you come ... But he never came! And then ..."

"Just a minute, Tara," said David, feeling a quite different kind of unease, "Beni *did* come. He came late. And he told me you walked right by him — Well no, let's get it right — you were as near as that wall, he says, and you didn't exactly pass him — you were going off *that* way, as he came from *here*.

And you cut him dead. Elvira saw him. She saw Beni go up the escalator and then you came down."

Tara was slowly sitting up as he spoke, her hands tightly gripping the arms of the chair, her eyes now open wide. "Oh no," she said, slowly and deliberately, "I did not see him, David."

They sat in silence for a while looking at the black night sky and the slender crescent moon.

"And I suppose Beni and Rita went off for a Chinese meal together after church this morning ... like we were all supposed to be doing?"

"Yes ... yes, I think they did ... But Tara, surely you don't think ...?"

"I don't know what I think," she said, standing up. "But I'm very, very tired and I think I'm going to bed."

On Monday Tara went looking for Beni at school, to apologize and to explain about not seeing him. He seemed rather unconvinced at first; no one likes to be made to look foolish. But he acknowledged that she had told him about her eyes on the Saturday afternoon — and he could remember very vividly the three boys, who had been the jeering witnesses of his discomfiture.

"You need to get those eyes tested, Ra," he told her. "It's no use trying patent eyedrops and wearing your sister's old specs. You need to really *do* something about it!"

"Yes," she said, "It's time I really *did* something."

CHAPTER FOUR

Mutiara's grandmother lived a month, more or less, with each of her sons in turn. She was a bent, gnarled old woman with solemn eyes and the bright red mouth that comes from too much betelnut chewing. She shared the girls' bedroom when she stayed with them, and the older girls found it irksome to be cross-examined when they came in late, and lectured on the way things used to be years ago. Their parents were sometimes sharp with Granny too; Tara suspected that her father would have preferred to forget about the tattered clothes and empty stomachs of his *kampung*[1] childhood in the Struggle for Independence. But when there was a death, or a wedding to be arranged, or a family crisis, Granny became the oracle to whom everyone listened, the "keeper of *adat*[2]" who knew exactly what must be done to fulfil their obligations to tradition and to the ancestors.

She listened thoughtfully as Tara unfolded her story one evening, chewing at her betelnut and

---

[1] Village, neighbourhood: a traditional community, usually poor.
[2] Tradition — a body of customs which the clan feel an obligation to follow, some of which are closely linked to belief in spirit and ancestor powers.

nodding her head. Pak and Ibu Sitompul had gone out, and so had David to a student meeting; Elvira was revising for a test, and the younger children were dozing in front of the television. No one took any notice of Mutiara and her grandmother, talking in low voices in one corner.

"David thinks I should go to the doctor," said Tara, "And so does Beni."

Granny shook her head derisively. "This isn't the sort of problem a doctor knows how to cure. And I don't suppose you've as much as hinted to that young man about Rita's part in it all." She looked shrewdly at her granddaughter. "So he's really not got much of the story, has he?"

Tara sighed. "You think it's Rita too, then, do you Gran? She does seem to have it in for me."

Granny nodded again and put her hand on Tara's knee. "You come with me when I go home to the *kampung* next week," she said. "The only thing to do when someone is playing the spirits against you is to go to someone stronger." She patted Tara's knee. "Come with me to the *dukun*, girl. We'll see you right." She shook her head. "There's no one plays around with my granddaughter and gets away with it!"

"I'm taking Tara home with me to the *kampung* tomorrow," Granny announced a few days later. Ibu Sitompul looked up in astonishment. It was very usual for Granny to take one of the little children for company. Like all Batak grandmothers she liked to have a small child around to cuddle and give sweets to; and Ibu Sitompul had been looking forward to handing over her second youngest, a naughty three year old. It was more unusual to take one of the older children. "I need some help to carry all my things," added Granny blithely.

Granny's home village was in a plantation area about sixty kilometres south of Medan. They caught one bus to Lubuk Pakam, then another to Kotarih, getting off before they reached the town to trudge the two kilometres down the side road to the *kampung*. Palmoil trees had given way to rubber trees, tall and graceful with dusky green leaves. A group of children were dawdling along ahead of them, on their way home from school; they stopped by the paddy field, just outside the village, to exchange insults with some boys who were taking waterbuffalo to bathe in the river. Some of the children were Mutiara's cousins, and there were shouts and exclamations as they turned and recognized the two travellers. Suddenly they were in the middle of a crowd. An older boy took their bags, Tara's uncle appeared from nowhere, and in no time they were there.

The *kampung* was basically a cluster of houses straddling the plantation road. The *dukun*'s house was almost the last in the row; a wooden house on stilts like the others, with a few pigs underneath, but there were signs of affluence in the new corrugated iron roof and the little porch at the front. Mutiara went there the following morning with her grandmother. A silent, grimfaced woman ushered them inside. The dark room was stuffy, and redolent with a slightly heady scent. Above the doors and in corners were strangely shaped stones and carved figures; the charms and tokens which ward off evil in so many rural (and even city) homes. An elderly man in a *sarung*[3] had been sitting in the porch as they approached the house, and Tara felt sure that it was the same man who came in now, in dark trousers and a white doctor's coat. He sat with his head bent as they explained the reasons for their visit, nodding at intervals, pausing to ask a question here and there. When Tara had finished her story there was a long silence. The old man's eyes were closed. Was he in a trance? Tara had heard, often enough, about the ancestor spirits who speak through *dukuns*, in a strange voice and an unknown language. She waited apprehensively. Was he asleep? Finally he gave a shudder, stood up, and went out into a back area.

He came back into the room a little later, bearing in one hand a small bottle and in the other a saucer, containing what looked like ashes. These he placed on the low table in front of them; then he sat down. His hand was resting over, but surely not

---

[3]Sheet of material with the ends sewn together, used as a wrap-around skirt by men or women around the house, or to sleep in instead of a top sheet.

touching, the saucer of ash. He muttered under his breath as his fingers moved over the saucer. When he removed them the ash seemed to have formed itself into a word — words — something almost — but not quite — familiar. Was it a verse from the Bible? Tara realized suddenly that the man was looking at her, asking a question.

"You want to be healed?" he asked. "And is it revenge you want, as well?"

Granny nodded, but "Oh no!" cried Tara. After all, there was no certainty that it was Rita who had caused her problems ... or anyone else for that matter. Like a fall off a cliff edge came the sudden awareness of the enormity of her suspicions, and just how slight, in fact, were the grounds for them.

The *dukun* shook the bottle and poured some of the medicine into a tiny glass.

"Drink this," he said, and she drank; the taste was bitter — repulsive even.

He pointed to the saucer with his chin. "Keep this by your bedside. The holy words must not be disturbed. Take one spoonful of the medicine each day till it is finished. But the ash must be kept until your sight is fully restored. May the great God bless you."

Mutiara solemnly took the saucer while her grandmother was counting out the money to pay for the consultation. The grimfaced woman showed them out. Slowly they stepped down from the porch and walked back along the road to Uncle's house.

CHAPTER FIVE

"No! No! ... Let me go!"

Mutiara twisted and turned, struggling to wrench herself free from the grip of ... With a start she awoke to find Elvira holding her wrists down tight against the bed. The other girl stared into her eyes for a full minute without speaking, then released her and sat up.

"Sorry, Vira," said Tara, rubbing her wrists, "It was another of those strange dreams."

Vira shrugged. "Just the usual. We're getting used to them." She felt about with her feet for the rubber thongs under the bed, and flip-flopped her way to the bathroom.

The monotonous chanting of the muezzin over the loudspeaker from the nearby mosque told Tara it was five o'clock; time to get up. She shivered as she slowly pulled herself into the present. She could never quite remember the dream, but the sense of fear lingered on — of being entrapped, coiled about with something horrible, of choking, suffocating. Not every night, as yet, but often enough — too often. She glanced at the saucer of ash, dusty now, its message indistinct, on a chest near the bed. Six months since she had been to the *dukun*; and already her nightmares were becoming "just the usual."

Slowly Tara trailed off for her *mandi*[1]. She jumped at the shock of cold water; dipper after dipperful, drenching, drowning, jolting her into wakefulness. Tingling all over she pummelled herself dry and pulled on her old working dress. She ought to throw that old saucer away; it was doing her no good at all. Her eyes were worse, if anything. It was no longer the vague, unprotected feeling of things creeping up on her from the side, that ill-defined sense of something wrong. Now she knew definitely that her sight was deteriorating; not just a narrowing of vision but an all-over blurring. Spirit lore and magic, black or white, seemed inappropriate. It was more a question, now, of having her eyes tested and admitting that she needed glasses.

Ibu Sitompul was thinking along much the same lines. She had noticed some while back that Tara was peering shortsightedly at everything. That morning as they set off for the market together she wondered just how far her daughter could see. Several times a *becak* crossed the end of the road, the driver pausing in his pedalling to glance their way in search of passengers. Ibu Sitompul watched and waited. Mutiara made no response. In the end her mother could bear it no longer and her hand shot up.

---
[1] Cold shower

"*Becak*!" she called, muttering crossly, "We've got to get there before tonight, you know!"

"Is there a *becak*?" asked Tara, screwing up her eyes against the dazzle of the low morning sun.

"Oh good, he's seen us. He's coming." Ibu Sitompul stood still by the side of the road to wait — but it was at least another minute before Tara said, "Here's one now!"

They negotiated the fare and clambered in. The driver wheeled round in a wide circle and re-mounted his bicycle.

"Tara," began her mother as they jolted along towards the market, "Did you really not see the *becak* until you said?" Then after a pause, "I'd seen it myself quite a bit before then." Another pause.

"I was looking straight into the sun," said Tara defensively, "But no," she admitted, "I didn't see it as soon as you did."

"You don't seem to be seeing too well these days," continued her mother. "We've all noticed you peering at us."

"Yes." Tara nodded. "I do need my eyes tested, Mum, don't I. I just wasn't sure, at first, that it was that sort of problem."

"Well," said Ibu Sitompul, "Your father reckons that we should take you to the eye hospital and have it done properly. There's a very good eye specialist. Dr. Sinaga. Trained in America. Your father met his brother-in-law the other day, by way of business. We'll make an appointment for you, and see if we can get you fixed up with some decent glasses."

"Yes Mum."

It seemed the matter was being taken out of her hands.

The eye hospital was attached to the University of North Sumatra, and it had a wide reputation. It was a drab and doleful building, or rather a complex of buildings around an open square, with covered walkways in between. Mutiara and her mother sat for an hour or so on a bench outside Dr. Sinaga's door. Eventually their turn came, and Tara was subjected to a wide and detailed array of tests. Finally Dr. Sinaga sat back and laid his black instrument down on the desk. He swivelled his chair round and began to rummage in a low drawer. Then he picked up a pen and made some cramped notes on the blue record card. He looked across at Ibu Sitompul over the rim of his glasses.

"Your daughter has glaucoma," he barked. "You should have come to me as soon as you became aware of the symptoms."

They looked at him dumbly.

With quick and efficient strokes he wrote out a prescription on a white form.

"This is for pilocarpine. Eye-drops. They must be taken every day without fail, unless I give notice of any change. I'll see you again in a month's time."

"Glaucoma?" faltered Tara. She wasn't shortsighted, then, and it didn't sound like what they called astygmatism.

"It's caused by pressure in this eye." He tapped her forehead above the right eye. "See where the pupil is bigger?"

Ibu Sitompul nodded doubtfully. The doctor pulled another pad towards him, a green one this time, and began scribbling again. "This is the prescription for her spectacles. Get them at any optician." He stamped both sheets and held them out. "It is imperative that the eye-drops be taken every day without fail. Come back next month and I will measure the pressure and adjust the dosage."

"Glaucoma," mused Tara as they walked slowly back along the corridor, "What's that? Is it a disease or what?"

"I don't know, Tara," said her mother with a worried frown. She was wondering what they had let themselves in for, with reappointments to measure this, that and the other at Rp.10,000 a time. "We'd better get the drops first, and then I'll talk to your father about the optician. He might know someone ... Maybe Vira's old frames would do. She was supposed to be shortsighted, but she never wears the things so you might as well have them."

"Mmm. Could do, I suppose."

She was glad, though, when her father insisted on buying her a new pair of glasses. They gave a little help to her vision and a big boost to her confidence. The tinted lenses were a protection and a disguise; for she was becoming obsessed with the fancy that her eyeballs were bulging, and the right eye, the painful one, was faintly tinged with pink.

Beni was sympathetic when he heard her story, and he agreed that the glasses improved her appearance. "You've been going round looking like an owl at midday," he said, hitting the nail on the head with a sledgehammer. "Not the pretty, perky pearl we used to know. And had you noticed, Ra, that one of your eyes is getting to be a bit bigger than the other?"

"Just the pupil, actually." Tara sighed. "That's one of the symptoms of glaucoma."

They were at the zoo with Ani and Yesaya, feeding peanuts to the monkeys. Ani threw the last few nuts to the baboons. "Ugly, bad-tempered beasts," she said, "but they need to eat too," and then they moved on to see the North Sumatran Tiger. He was pacing to and fro, round and round the narrow confines of his enclosure, back and forth, back and forth, in endless frustration. Just like me, thought Tara, pacing about, fears and worries inside my brain.

"He's sick, too, poor thing!" she cried, squeezing Beni's arm, "Look at the way he's limping! That leg looks so stiff and sore."

"Needs seeing to, doesn't it?" Beni shrugged. "We've given two tigers to New York zoo, and we can't even manage to keep *one* healthy ourselves!"

"Let's go for a drink — I'm so parched I'll collapse," suggested Yesaya, and they turned away. But Tara looked back over her shoulder, with fellow feeling, at the pacing tiger.

Beni sat in silence for a long time, contemplating his Seven-Up. Ani, who taught in Sunday School, was debating the pros and cons of a Sunday School outing to the zoo. "We'll give peanuts and bananas to the monkeys and the deer," said Yesaya with a grin, "And we'll throw the naughty children to the crocodiles!"

They all laughed.

Beni turned his bottle round and round abstractedly.

"You'd better keep up with those eye-drops, Ra," he said suddenly.

"Oh, I am!" Fear gripped again at her stomach with icy fingers. "I don't want to go blind!"

"Blind!" Beni looked up quickly. "It's as serious as that, then?" He drummed on the table with his fingers. "Poor Ra!" His hand closed on hers for a brief moment before he beckoned the waitress over and made a show of paying for the drinks. "Are we going to see the crocodiles, then?" he asked. "Who shall we throw to them this time?"

CHAPTER SIX

Mutiara used the eye-drops daily at first, and in different ways she tried, unobtrusively, to assess the effect on her vision. There seemed to be little change, however. The specialist was very noncommittal at her next appointment, nodding and tutting to himself and making tiny notes on her record card before writing out a prescription for more eye-drops. She wanted to ask if there were signs of progress, but she was paralyzed by the hospital aura; the long still corridors, the secretive nurses, strange smells, and all the quietly menacing paraphernalia — black, chrome, white, grey. So she sat passively like a dumb animal submitting to the treatment of its keepers. The doctor made no comment, beyond reminding her to take the eye-drops each day and to come back after a month. He was the most frightening of them all, with his stooping shoulders, his harsh voice and those cool, detached eyes which penetrated her body but ignored her person.

Tara's father was becoming increasingly disillusioned with the hospital.

"How long is all this going to go on for?" he asked Ibu Sitompul when the third visit had produced only another prescription and a further appointment for a month ahead. He had been prepared for a high consultation fee — initially — and perhaps an expensive pair of glasses. But now the process seemed endless.

"This doctor's on to a good thing, if you ask me," he grumbled. "Take the drops every day and come back next month to measure the pressure! Not bad at Rp.10,000 a ten-minute visit and Rp.2,000 a bottle! As if we'd nothing else to spend our money on!"

Ibu Sitompul nodded. She was only too well aware of the strains of seeing David through university and four other children through school. Not to mention the three youngest, who were constantly catching colds and fevers and needing vitamin injections from the clinic. If only her husband could realize the struggle she had stretching her meagre housekeeping money round a month's meals, when all the time the price of rice was going up, kerosene for the stove was going up, and the wage of a civil servant — or what she saw of it — barely keeping up with them.

"And I notice her sight's not getting any better, is it?" continued Pak Sitompul. "Worse, in fact. I can't bear to look at her! Dark glasses, stumbling over things, wandering along the road in that vacant, dopey way as if she doesn't know where she's going. She'll be blind before we get to the end of it, I tell you!" He sat down heavily on the bed. "Whatever have we done, to deserve all this?"

So the fourth appointment was quietly forgotten — and the next. Tara had kept her last prescription, and when the bottle was empty she went back to the same pharmacy and asked them to renew it. Each bottle lasted longer now, for the simple reason that she was becoming very haphazard in taking the drops. It all seemed so pointless when they were clearly doing no good. Like the saucer of ash they had failed ... and yet ... and yet ... She was fearful of the consequences if she stopped taking them completely. Just as she feared the consequences of throwing away the saucer.

Just keep on living — mechanically — like a robot. Get up, wash, dress, help with the chores, school, home, bed — not thinking, not feeling, numbing the pain. Slowly she closed in on herself. The nightmares came once or twice a week now, and most other nights her worries paced in her brain like the tiger at the zoo — in spite of all her efforts to stop them.

No way out, no way out, walls and bars on all sides.

What have I done that this should happen to me? Where shall I turn? The dukun's no good, doctor's no good. What if I go blind? What then? An empty vista stretched out before her; barren desert; the rest of her life. The only blind people she could think of were those from the hostel; disgorged in busloads at a different point each day to shuffle from house to house with a bundle of doormats and brooms to sell, and a ragged child to lead them by the hand and check their money. She pictured herself as shabby, middle-aged, old, with a little niece in tow. Not her own child, of course, because she could never marry. Who would marry her now? Beni was a memory. He had not been near for weeks; concerned, yes, but far away. Even the lifts home had dwindled and died long before the end of term. Not all his fault, perhaps. She knew she had been prickly and proud.

But when daylight came she slammed the lid down, tight, on her mind and heart in order to survive. Until one Sunday afternoon when David found her on the back porch, sitting dejectedly on the broken old chair, pulling bits of rattan to pieces as the tears drizzled down her face. Poor Tara, he hated to see her like this; woebegone, plain, with straggly hair and crumpled dress, she who not so long ago had been so pretty and trim. The hard knot of pity tightened in his chest with almost physical pain. Pity — and shame. He did not want to have a blind sister. But he could not speak of these things.

"I've just got back from the committee meeting," he said. "Been planning the Long Walk to Brastagi. Should be good ... Transport's OK. Pak Sembiring's coming — he's the leader responsible for the youth group now. And Pak Peranginangin's bringing his truck. The *pendeta*[1] can't come — but we've asked Pendeta James Stephens to speak at the service after the Walk, so

---
[1] Minister

CHAPTER SIX

we've got his jeep too. We'll drive as far as that point ... what's it called? You know the place. And then walk the rest of the way ... You'll come, won't you, Tara? Vira's said she's definitely coming."

Tara blinked, but made no move to wipe her tearstained face. "No, I couldn't, Dave! I've not been to youth group for such a long time."

"Doesn't matter. Good time to start again."

"And I couldn't walk all that way! ... Not as I am now!"

"Yes, you could! Nothing wrong with your legs, is there? Anyway, you could stick with the cars and ride all the way if you wanted to — wait for us at the top with the food!"

"I don't even know when it is."

"Oh, it's very soon now, next Thursday. It's that holiday — you know — Idul Adha or something — when the Muslims remember how Abraham sacrificed Ishmael (or so they say). You must have noticed the kids tethered by the roadside — there are six outside the post office keeping the grass short while they fatten them up for slaughter!"

But of course Tara had not noticed; there was little she *did* notice these days. David tried another tack. "Beni should be there," he said. "You'd like to see him again, wouldn't you? He hasn't been round for ages, and this is your last chance before he goes off to university to Jakarta!"

"Oh don't talk about Beni," snapped Tara. "Better ask *him* if he wants to see *me* again! No one wants to know a blind girl!"

CHAPTER SEVEN

The Medan sun shone fierce and bright on the morning of Idul Adha; an empty promise, for the rainy season was just beginning. Already the sky was overcast as the little convoy drew up at the corncob stands that marked the starting point of the Long Walk. There was the hint of a chill in the air; and with a laughing, scrambling, shivering clamour, the whole flock swooped down round the huge cauldrons which bubbled smokily over wood-packed stoves. Thirty pairs of eyes followed the two wool-muffled old women as they brought out cob after steaming cob until all were satisfied.

The rough stalls, bare plank-tables under palm-thatched roofs, formed a parapet round the outer edge of a wide hairpin bend. Beneath them the ground fell away steeply; David, astride a bench, looked down over the tops of tall trees to the fuzzy green patchwork below. Dark cloud-shadows moved slowly, amoeba-like, across the plain, fingering clumps of banana palms and red-roofed houses, absorbing flashes of burnt gold paddy stubble, blackening the green trees and the muddy brown, newly ploughed fields.

"Should we risk it, then?" asked Beni. "What's

your assessment of the weather, Professor? Will we make it to the top or will the rain get us first?"

He was sitting facing the road, leaning back against the table with his hands in his pocket, legs stretched out in front of him, immaculate as ever in navy blue jeans and smart new track shoes.

"Oh, we'll make it," said David. "It'll rain some time today, that's for sure, but I think we've a few hours ahead of us yet. What do you think, Pak James?"

The English minister took a final bite of corn before tossing the empty husk in the bin.

"I'd say it's a great day for walking," he said. "Not too hot, just a slight breeze to help you along." He paused. "Of course, it's easy for me to talk — I'll be driving up so I wouldn't get wet anyway! But we can always come back for the stragglers if need be. In fact we can take some passengers all the way if some of you don't feel like walking?" He glanced across at Mutiara, who smiled and nodded.

"You'll come in the car too, Vira, won't you," she said.

"Oh, no, I'm walking!" said Vira, springing up with a determined air. "Not much point in going on a Long Walk if you ride all the way!"

"That's the spirit!" said Yesaya, who was bustling round trying to get them all started. "We'll have you in the front, Vira, shall we?"

But Vira looked alarmed, and sat down again hurriedly next to Beni. It was David who took the lead, with another friend Tomo, a law student who sometimes sang with the group. They stepped out briskly, followed closely by a crowd of high school boys and a few of the more energetic girls. Beni was further back, strolling at a leisurely pace with Elvira on one side and Rita, stunningly attractive in a crisp red shirt, on the other. A straggle of girls were behind them, and right at the back a group of sullen-faced boys who did not usually attend the youth group. Yesaya brought up the rear, with his brother Yahya, ready to gather up any who fell by the wayside.

The drivers lingered over their Cokes to give the walkers time to make some headway. Ani had elected to keep Tara company, along with two other girls who formed the catering committee. They rode up in Pak Sembiring's car, the most comfortable, while the cooking pots followed in the truck, and the food in the missionary's jeep. The line was already stretched out as they passed, like badly strung beads, with ever widening gaps between the little knots of hikers. Rita walked closely beside Beni, their heads bent together in some absorbing conversation, while Vira swung her arms nonchalantly, the outsider, tagging along beside them. Ani glanced at her friend's face as they drove by the trio, but she seemed not to notice; her eyesight was too weak by now, perhaps, to distinguish people from behind.

Mutiara was lost in thought, as it happened, reviewing the scene at the cornstalls. Beni had travelled up in a different vehicle, and she had not known he was there till she felt his hand on her shoulder.

"Here, Ra," he had said gently, "this one's young and tender." He smiled as he gave her the corncob and guided her out through the crush. "Let's sit down and have a talk. I've not seen you for ages."

But what was there to talk about? Her absorbing interest these days, her eyesight, she would not discuss.

"When do you leave for Jakarta?" she began.

"How's the old eyes, then?" he asked at the same time. They laughed, but before they could begin again the others had crowded round onto the benches and the conversation became public property. They had sat in a row; Pendeta James, David, Beni, Mutiara, Elvira, munching corn and giggling over Beni's account of his shopping for "Jakarta clothes." Tara sighed, wondering if that was the nearest she would get to seeing him alone.

The recreation site was almost deserted, surprisingly so on a public holiday; the threatening skies had deterred all but the hardy. Whirling mist-clouds shrouded the mountain peaks, and the weather was distinctly cold. They parked the cars near one of the larger shelters and pulled on sweaters before setting to work. Pendeta James and Pak Sembiring unrolled the long woven mats to cover the concrete floor, while Pak Peranginangin helped the girls to carry in and unpack the plates, glasses, pots and kettles. The food had all been cooked beforehand; it was merely a matter of setting out the gigantic tubs of rice and the many side dishes; fried noodles, noodle soup, tiny dried fish fried with peanuts and chillies, vegetables cooked with fishballs and chicken livers, hot stewed beef, and bunch after bunch of bananas. Huge kettles were set to boil on two kerosene stoves. Then they could sit back and wait for the first of the hikers to arrive.

"Tell us about your family, Pak James," said Ani, "Do you just have the two children?"

"Just two."

"Boys or girls?"

"Two boys; Mark and Daniel; three years and one year old."

"And how do you like Indonesia?"

"Very much."

"What do you like about Indonesia?"

What indeed! After being asked this question two thousand times, he ought to have a ready answer. Jim wondered where to start.

"Well ..." He waved his hand vaguely in the direction of the mountain top. "It's a beautiful country, isn't it? Mountains, rivers, paddyfields, all that lush green and gold."

"And what have you passed?" asked Tara. "Did you do five years of theology, like Pendeta Saragih?"

"No, just two years at a Bible College. But I had studied physics at university before that."

"Oh." Ani nodded sympathetically. "And did you fail your exams?"

Jim smiled. "No, I passed. I have a B.Sc. in physics, and I worked in industry for a while before I went to Bible College."

"Did you think it would be easier, then, being a pendeta?" asked Tara, feeling at a loss to explain the shift in career.

"No, I didn't," said Jim quietly. "I felt that God was calling me to come out here. Everything else followed from that."

"Oh." The girls smiled in polite disbelief.

"Here they come now," said Ani, nodding towards the entrance as David and Tomo came through the gateway. She jumped up to get them a drink. "They'll be thirsty after all that."

"Hi!" said David, flinging himself down on the mat and taking the glass of sweet tea. "Thanks a lot, Ani." He gulped it down and wiped his mouth. "It was a good walk, but it was only the promise of a long drink at the end that kept us going for that last bit."

"I'm afraid we got a bit ahead," said Tomo, cradling his drink. "Quite a bit ahead, actually — but the others will be here before too long."

They came in dribs and drabs, red-faced, dishevelled, stumbling a little over the last few hummocks — thirsty and hungry but exhilarated — and very, very glad to sit down. Some of the girls were hobbling a bit in tight, smart shoes. Tara watched as a red-blue splodge came wearily across the grass towards them. The girl was limping slightly, leaning heavily on her boyfriend; both moved awkwardly, as if exhausted. They came closer. With a start she realized that it was Beni and Rita. He led her to the platform edge of the shelter, and bent solicitously to help ease off her shoes. Tara turned away, eyes smarting, and busied herself with the rice plates. Mechanically she bowed her head for the formal prayer of thanksgiving, then grabbed up a rice spoon and began ladling mindlessly; scoop, plonk, pass it on, scoop, plonk, pass it on, smile and scoop, pass it on. Eventually she took her own plate to where Ani was sitting with David at the back of the shelter.

"What do you think, Tara?" said David. "We were just wondering if we could manage a side trip to the hot springs on the way down."

"Mmm."

"I can't see us getting there," said Ani. "Look, it's spotting with rain now! We'll have a downpour soon. Just wait!"

"Mmm," said Tara again, scarcely hearing. Round and round in her mouth went the dry rice, round and round, and still she could not swallow it. She bit on the hot green chilly and let the fire sweep through, catching at her throat.

"This *rendang* is far too hot," said Ani, waving her spoon of spicy beef and looking with concern at Tara's red eyes. "Too much chilly."

Tara nodded.

The few spots of rain had turned to a steady

drizzle. Yesaya was discussing the "open air" service with Pendeta James.

"We'd better have it here in the shelter," he suggested. "It's big enough. We'll have to clear the food away first, of course."

"Sounds fine," agreed Jim.

Tara went to help the cooks, moving quickly and silently, gathering up dirty plates, scooping banana skins into the bins, stacking everything away neatly in cardboard cartons which were stowed away in the truck.

Beni, with Rita, was in the middle of a laughing group.

"So here I am," he sighed tragically, "Enjoying my last taste of fresh mountain air before I sink into the squelch of sticky Jakarta!"

"He doesn't look too concerned, though, does he," laughed Yesaya, "about his imminent departure for the Mother City."

"Well, you know, really I'm ..."

"Really you can't wait to get there," wailed Rita. "You just don't care how much we'll miss you."

"And I'll miss you too, Sweet Face," said Beni. "But you've got to move on, haven't you — got to keep moving!"

Tara took a songsheet from Yesaya and sat down as far away from the others as she could. She leaned back against a pillar with her eyes shut and let the service wash over her. *Move on, then Beni, move on, and leave us all behind you. We're not worth clinging on to.*

"... He was born blind ..."

Like her own name, the word leapt out at her from the droning background at the edge of her mind.

"And so Jesus had to explain to them that, No, it wasn't this man's fault, nor his parents' fault that he was born blind. It wasn't a punishment for wrongdoing. No. God had a purpose for him in his blindness, and that purpose was that God should be glorified when Jesus healed him."

Jesus healed the blind man. She repeated the words to herself. *It wasn't his fault he was blind; he hadn't done anything wrong. Jesus healed him.*

"And see how gradually God opens the man's spiritual eyes too. The Pharisees say that Jesus is a sinner. Well, they are the people who should know! But he sticks to the faith he has so far; 'Whether he is a sinner I don't know,' he tells them, 'One thing I know, that though I was blind, now I see.'"

What was the story now? Jesus spat on the ground and made clay, and he put it on the man's eyes. And when he washed it off he could see. Tara closed her eyes again and tried to imagine a mudpack on the lids. Pendeta James was still speaking.

"Now he goes a bit further. God doesn't listen to sinners. If this man were not from God he could do nothing. So our friend stands up boldly in front of these tough leaders, the Pharisees, and he says, Jesus must be from God!"

Though I was blind, now I see. Tara deliberately allowed herself, for a moment, to sink down into that sense of utter hopelessness and despair that had engulfed her, it seemed, for so long. *Now I see.* Lifting her head she mentally rose up from the swamp.

"So he says to Jesus, 'Who is this Son of Man, that I may believe in him?' And Jesus says, ' I am the one.' And immediately the man responds by worshipping Jesus. *Now* he's got there!"

Of course, you don't get that sort of thing these days. Or do you? The dukuns reckon to heal people, so why not Jesus? Are there Christian dukuns? That one in the kampung seemed to use a Bible — or Bible verses ... But somehow ...

"And how many people are going round without even wearing glasses, but in spiritual terms they are totally blind? Because that's where it really matters in the long run. And only Jesus, by the Holy Spirit, can open those spiritually blind eyes. Only ..."

But Tara was no longer listening. She was wondering how to get talking with the missionary after the service.

There was no time, however, for more than a mad dash through the now torrential rain to the waiting cars for the steamy drive home. David, Tara and Elvira were in the jeep for the journey downhill. As they reached the house, Tara leaned over to the front.

"What's your address, again?" she asked. "I'd

like to come and see your wife, and the children, one day."

"Yes, do," said Jim. "Anytime. 'Bye now," he called as they hurried across the plank and in at the gate.

Yes do, he thought as he put the car into gear and drove off. *Poor Tara, I hope she didn't take my talk personally. I hadn't realized she'd be coming today.*

CHAPTER EIGHT

The following week Mutiara and Elvira called round at the missionary's house.

"Why, hello! Nice to see you." Pak James beamed as he ushered them into the small square sitting room. "This is Mutiara," he introduced them, "And her sister Elvira. They were on the Long Walk last week and they said they'd like to get to know you."

"Glad you could come." said Ibu Stephens. "We've seen each other at church sometimes, haven't we?" She left them sitting and went off to make drinks. It was half past five, almost time to be getting the children's tea. She gave them a banana each and hoped that would keep them going.

Mutiara looked at the long brown Batik curtains, and the dark-framed pictures on the wall. A slender vase of orchids brightened the low rattan table. Foreigners always had rattan furniture — the sort that other people kept outside on the verandah.

A small boy ran in giggling and pumped their hands vigorously up and down. "Selamat sore.

Selamat *sore!*" His brother, Daniel, was being clingy, hiding his face in Mummy's skirt.

"What are you eating?" asked Tara, trying to be friendly. "Pisang, ya?"

"Pisang!" said Mark proudly, waving his banana, and the girls laughed.

"Oh — he can speak Indonesian!" said Vira, pinching his cheek. "Clever!"

Mark rubbed the red patch on his cheek and looked at his mother.

"Elvira wants to make friends with you, darling."

Jim excused himself and went off to take a shower in preparation for a meeting.

"How many children do you have?" asked Mutiara. The visiting ritual began.

"Just two children."

"Boys or girls?"

"Two boys. Three years old and thirteen months."

"How long have you been married?"

"Seven years."

"Oh." Seven years and only two children. "Family planning?"

Oh dear, thought Ruth, *don't start asking me what method.* "And how about you, Mutiara? How many brothers and sisters in your family?"

"Nine in the family. I am number two, and she is number three. Five boys, one of them dead, and four girls."

"Have a drink, won't you." Ruth gestured to the

glasses and the girls took a cautious sip. "Daniel, NO!" Ruth quickly rescued her glass. "Here, Mummy will get you a drink of juice."

"Can I have another banana?" asked Mark.

"No, love, you won't want your tea."

"What is England like?" asked Tara.

How do you sum up a country in a sentence? "Well ... It's colder than here, of course. No Mark, don't climb on the wall. Come inside and play ... Our hot season is more like the cooler, mountain areas of Indonesia — like Brastagi." They shivered.

"What's it *like*, though, living there?" Tara thought of some of the shots she had seen on television; men in thick coats getting in and out of cars; football crowds; soldiers and barbed wire in Northern Ireland; were Charlie's Angels English, or was that America? The BeeGees. "Does everyone in England have a car?" she asked finally. "Do they have *becaks* there?"

Ruth laughed. "No, no *becaks*." She unclasped a hymnbook from her toddler's hand and gave him a wooden block, which he threw across the floor. *Why doesn't she send them both out the back?* wondered Tara irritably. *Doesn't she have anyone to look after them?* She thought of her own, shabbier, home, where small children would never be allowed to intrude on a social visit. It was a relief when Pak James came back into the room, a briefcase in his hand. He smiled apologetically at the visitors.

"I'm sorry, I have to go out now, to a Bible study. ... But perhaps I can give you a lift?"

The two girls sprang to their feet. "Come again, won't you," said Ruth, and they smiled noncommittally.

They did go back, however, the next week ... and the next. It was a month before Tara felt able to broach the subject that concerned her.

"I don't see very well," she began.

"I know," said Ruth quietly.

"I have glaucoma."

"I'm sorry, Mutiara. Have you had it long? Are you having treatment?"

Tara began to explain how the illness had started, and about the visits to the eye specialist.

"I don't really know what glaucoma is," said Ruth. "But we have a book that may help." She disappeared for a moment and came back with a black book which she thumbed through to find a page which had diagrams of eyes.

"Are you a nurse?"

"No. Teacher. But this book is fairly simple. We use it if the children get sick — sort of first aid. Glaucoma ... starts with not seeing things from the side, and sometimes pain in the eye?" Tara nodded. "Oh! You need to take eye-drops every day." She looked up.

"Yes, I used to," said Tara, "But they don't do any good."

"Oh ... but it says here ..." Ruth paused, looking anxious. "It says if you don't take the drops every

CHAPTER EIGHT 59

day — maybe for the rest of your life — then you could get worse — even go blind!"

Tara looked at her in horror.

"And you are still seeing the specialist? It says here you need to measure the pressure regularly."

Tara slumped in the chair. "It's all so expensive." Something these Westerners, with their big jeep and expensive toys scattered all over, would know nothing about. And there was something else she wanted to ask. Vira was beginning to stand up, but the elder girl broke in quickly:

"What do you think of *dukuns*?"

"*Dukuns*? You mean people who claim to heal, using kampung medicine? Using magic and spirit power?"

"*Dukuns*, yes. Do you think it's all right to go to them?"

"No, I don't, Mutiara. It's wrong and it's dangerous. What is it you say here? Powers of Darkness? Keep away from powers of darkness. Christians should walk in the light."

"Well, I went to the *dukun* once, a long time ago." She shrugged. "But I don't think he's any good, you're right. It didn't work."

"You went to the *dukun*. About your eyes?"

"Yes, I ..." Slowly, bit by bit, Tara unfolded the story; the feeling of oppression, Granny, the kampung *dukun*, the saucer of ash. "But I had these awful dreams! ... Still get them, but not so much now ... It's ..." She shuddered. "Frightening! But I don't believe in it. Granny wants me to try again. But it doesn't work. I could throw that saucer away, even. The words don't show anymore." She stopped, awkwardly, aware that the missionary was frowning at her. Was it such a terrible thing she had done?

Ruth sat back in consternation. She really must get fixed up for some more sessions with the language teacher. Buying carrots and fish in the market was no preparation for this sort of conversation. She was sure she had missed half of it — and the half she had grasped filled her with dismay. With a gulp she sought for the right words.

"Tara love, it's not just that the *dukun* might not manage to heal you. *Dukuns* do, sometimes, have power. But it's a dangerous power. There's a real danger of being — tied — by this connection with the evil spirits — of being *bound* I mean. You should smash that saucer! Throw it right away! And you need to see the doctor, and start taking those drops again."

They sat for a moment in silence. Tara could feel, almost tangibly, the walls of a dank, dark prison closing in about her.

"Shall we pray about it?"

"Yes, please."

Later Ruth stood by the gate as the two girls walked down the road, arms linked. Tara walked clumsily, adrift in her depression. She should have gone to their own pendeta — these Westerners didn't really understand. But Pendeta Saragih was far too busy, she was sure, to sit and talk with a teenager. He'd likely tear a strip off her, for not going to youth group or something. And anyway, she remembered him saying in a sermon that the *dukuns did* have power, but that Christians weren't allowed to go to them. Wasn't there *anyone* who could help?

"Oh Tara!" muttered Vira crossly, pulling her back from the ditch. "Do be careful, can't you!"

"Well *tell* me, can't you!" she snapped. "You're supposed to be *helping* me, aren't you?"

Ruth watched their ungainly progress to the end of the road, then turned, eyes closed, and groped her way along the path into the house, wondering how it felt to be going slowly blind.

CHAPTER NINE

Worst of all was the boredom.

The new term had begun, and everyone seemed busy. David was on campus most of the time, in lectures, in the library or at student Christian meetings. Vira was throwing herself with unusual enthusiasm into her final year of high school, and in her spare time taking private English lessons. Mutiara's old class had dispersed now; some like Beni to study in Java, some still in Medan, scattered around the city's eight universities and innumerable colleges. A few were working; a larger number were looking for work — not very hopefully or very actively — waiting patiently while their parents sifted through long lists of relatives for one who might, somewhere, have a position which a bright high school leaver might fill.

Ani had started on a secretarial course at a college in the town centre which specialized in English language business studies. They had planned at one time to go together; but shorthand and typing were out of the question now, as far as Tara was concerned. She had barely scraped through the school leaving exams, after struggling increasingly, during those last few months, to cope with the closely printed textbooks. What could she do? She scrubbed clothes, she helped with the cooking, less often now and rather clumsily, she babyminded. She began to visit the missionary family, in part to improve her English, though when it came to it she tended to stick to Indonesian. Ruth tried to encourage her to read simple story books to Mark, not realizing that her eyesight was no longer up to it, and feeling irritated when Tara put the books aside and played silly giggling games instead.

She had not said anything, yet, to Pak James about his sermon on healing the blind man, though he often asked her about her eyes, and the rehearsed questions often hovered, unspoken, on her lips.

"Are you taking the eye-drops?" he would ask, and she would nod her head. She had been back again, with her mother, to the eye hospital, and faced the cold disapproval of the specialist who informed them, of course, that her condition had deteriorated. But her headaches were less severe, now that she was taking the drops regularly. Coming home with Vira in the *becak* that day from the missionary's house, she felt almost happy.

They found a houseful waiting for them; an aunt and uncle who had come with two sons and a daughter to make arrangements for a trip to Lake Toba for a big family wedding the following week. Tradition dictated who should do what, and Aunt Rini was armed with a sheaf of photocopies showing who was related in what way to the bride, what gift they should therefore give, and what their duties would be at the ceremony. Ibu Sitompul must take charge of cooking the pork for the enormous feast.

"Your daughter will help."

"Not Mutiara," put in Pak Sitompul.

"No, of course not," said Aunt impatiently. "Elvira will help. And you can bring along David. There's no room in the car for the younger children — they must stay at home. Mutiara will look after them."

"Mustn't have the Eyesore at the wedding," muttered Tara under her breath, "Might bring bad luck. They might end up having a blind baby!" She glanced at her father but he looked quickly away. Pak Sitompul seemed to have given up on his daughter. When he spoke to her at all it was harshly, as if he blamed her for her illness. Mostly he avoided her, like an unwelcome friend to whom he owed money.

"And I've been making enquiries about the Blind School," continued Aunt Rini in a brisk voice. "I happened to meet one of the Board members." She took a sip of sweet tea and looked round the hushed room. "I can't understand why you've not done something about it before now!" Pak Sitompul coughed and looked down at the floor. "It's a very good place — almost in the country. Fresh air. Healthy. She can study Braille, and they do occupational training — little plots of land where they grow things, making rattan baskets, doormats — you know the sort of stuff. She wouldn't do that, of course. I said to Ibu Tobing, I said, she's a high school graduate, I said, she can learn Braille, and later on she can go to that special training college in Jakarta and learn to teach in a Blind School." She took another drink of tea while the family looked on, stunned. "The big thing is, she'll be learning Braille." She beamed triumphantly. "And living in the hostel, of course. Home at weekends." She sat back and smoothed down her skirt with an air of satisfaction.

Tara gaped at her, appalled. Learning Braille! Off in a hostel way out of town! Packed away!

"But I'm not blind!" Almost she choked on the words, backing away as all eyes turned towards her, their message unmistakeably clear, even to her dimmed sight. "I'm *not blind*!" she protested. Her hands fumbled behind her back for the handle of the bedroom door, and she escaped inside, flinging herself on the bed and grabbing at the pillow to stifle the sobs which would keep coming.

But of course it was the obvious solution.

Once the suggestion had been made it seemed inevitable that she should be enrolled at the Blind School. One step followed another, inexorably. The visit, the application, her father persuading them to take her immediately. Packing her bags, driving out along the busy Siantar Road, with the heavy, thudding roar of traffic noises hammering away at her head and a sick, leaden feeling weighing down her stomach. Staring numbly, unseeing, as grey factory walls gave way to black tyre stalls, and then to watermelons, piled high by the roadside, and to tall dark trees, looming over the road, a high gloomy tunnel stretching forever.

The rain was starting as the bus stopped. David grabbed Tara's bag, her mother took her arm, and between them they bustled her across the road and in at the gate before the early warning drops became a deluge. Behind her the beating water formed a white, sheet-iron wall, cutting off the past. Before them stood a short, stocky woman with a smiling face and outstretched hand.

"Good afternoon. I'm Ibu Tobing. Welcome to the Blind School."

They sipped tea in the bare entrance hall, searching for small talk and waiting for the rain to ease off. Ibu Tobing called for one of the girls to show Tara round. There was little to see. They passed through a long dining room and into a dark kitchen. The student, Evi, stood at the open doorway and gestured with her chin towards the other buildings grouped around the square.

"Church over there. Have to go. No choice. Classrooms there. That's offices and the boys' dormitories up above. Quite separate." She turned abruptly and started up the steep stone steps. "Girls' dorms on this side. Come on."

Tara stumbled after her. The room was plain and sparsely furnished, the beds grouped in pairs with locked cupboards between them. On the dirty cream wall was a large calendar and a cross-stitched picture; going up to it she could make out a black cross entwined with pink and white flowers and a text, *God with us*. A much older girl was bundled up in a *sarung* on one of the beds, lying with her back to the door.

"Wake up!" said Evi. "Here's our new roommate." She walked over to the bed and gave the girl a shake, pulling her round to face the room. Tara took in the one glazed, sightless eye, and the hollow, sucked-in shell where the other should have been, and she clutched at the door, fighting nausea. The blind girl sat up and stretched out her hand in not quite the right direction.

"Hello. My name's Elli."

Tara crept forward to place her reluctant hand in the sturdy brown one.

"Mutiara. Hello."

"You're not blind, are you?" said Elli. "Or, at least you're not used to it. I can tell by the way you move."

"No. I've got glaucoma. My sight is very poor, but I hope I won't go blind." Tara stared at the wall as she spoke, at the window, at the floor; anywhere but at the ugly, smiling face before her.

"It's hard at first, but you'll learn." Tara flinched as Elli patted her arm. "I hope you won't go blind, Mutiara. But you'll learn new skills, you know. God will help you. We can help each other."

She reached over to the cupboard and picked up a pair of dark glasses. "These are my disguise," she laughed. "Make me look pretty!"

She would never be that. Her face was drawn up, somehow, pulled towards that awful hole which the glasses did not completely hide. But it was possible, now, to look at her without that sick revulsion.

Tara quickly unpacked her few things, and Evi led her back along the corridor.

"Not much wrong with *your* sight, is there?" asked Tara. "Why are you in here?"

"Infection of the cornea. Doesn't it show? I can't see at all out of one eye. The pain was incredible!" She shuddered. "When it stopped I couldn't see. Now they say the other might get infected. But I don't think so. I don't need to be here, really. Had a big row at home and they sent me off."

"Oh?"

"Want to stop me going to late parties and things. They think this is the way to do it. Lock me up with old Tobing! That's not what they said, of course." She tossed her head back. She was a very pretty girl, pale with delicate features, and the tinted glasses added to her attractiveness. "But there's a whole kampung over that back wall, and a gang of boys with Hondas. I'll introduce you one time if you like. Might get taken into town one night."

"Mmm." Tara was not sure if she wanted to be whisked off on the back of a motorbike, with someone she did not know, to a place she could barely see. "Don't they try it on a bit — knowing we can't see too well, I mean?"

"So what! I mean to have some fun out of life!" Evi clenched her fists, and her voice for a moment was angry and bitter. "They can't just ruin my life and not expect me to fight back!"

Who were "they", Tara wondered. Her parents? Her eyes? God? The spirits?

Ibu Sitompul was standing in the doorway saying her goodbye to the warden. David was chatting to the gardener in the drive. No — it was another blind student. She could tell by the lopsided set of his shoulders, even before she saw his face. They walked to the gate together and stood waiting for the bus.

"Rudi will show you round," said David. "You remember him, don't you? We saw him at Taladan last Christmas."

Tara remembered the big youth rally, and the group who sang Silent Night so beautifully, and herself thinking how stupid to have a blind man with them, spoiling the look of the thing — and then his solo, deep and compelling, and the way they had all hummed the tune, over and over on the way home. And already then she had had glaucoma; only she didn't know it.

"Do you sing, Tara?" he asked, as he showed her round the garden later. "We have a lot of fun in the choir here."

"No, I don't sing."

But she agreed to go along to the choir practice that evening, to give it a try.

CHAPTER TEN

It was a relief, in some ways, when Tara went to the Blind School. Not that they wanted to be rid of her, David assured himself, but the atmosphere at home was certainly lighter without her brooding, doleful presence. There was a sense now, that something was being done for her, even if it meant accepting the worst, and a freedom to be happy without feeling guilty in the face of Tara's unhappiness. David himself was fully occupied these days, mostly with Christian Union activities. He was prayer secretary now of the group in his faculty, much to his father's disgust.

"There's far too many of these prayer groups around these days," grumbled Pak Sitompul. "Holding meetings all over the place, with their choruses and their big Bibles and their holy smiles. Acting like no one else is a Christian but them!"

He had just come in late, from a stormy elders' meeting at the church, and he was irritated beyond measure by the sight of his son sitting with a Bible in front of him.

"Made me ashamed tonight! Here's everyone slamming the prayer fellowships, and my own son's involved in running one of them!"

"Oh no, Dad!" protested David. "The Christian Union's quite different! Everyone knows that!" He paused. "But I don't see what's wrong about the fellowships either. It can't be that bad, can it, just to study the Bible and to pray together?"

His father snorted. "What's wrong with the church service every Sunday, that's what I want to know! Why do you need to go running off to all these other things as well, that are right outside the church?" He slammed home the bolts on the door and reached through the window to close the shutters tight. "Fanatical, that's what!"

David sighed. The Sunday services, slow moving, solemn and remote, were a totally different experience from the interdenominational fellowship groups.

"Ever since I became a church elder everything has gone wrong," Pak Sitompul complained. "First it was all that trouble at the office. Then your little brother takes a fever and dies. Now your sister's going blind. And all you can do is waste your time praying, when you ought to be studying!"

"Dad, I ..."

"*Your* time and *my* money! We'll see if *that* gets you a good job at the end of it!"

The bedroom door slammed behind him.

I should go off to Lake Toba and join a dope ring, thought David. Or *get a girl pregnant*. He closed his Bible. *But I won't. I'll go to bed instead, and tomorrow I'll meet my blind sister and take her to drink tea with the English missionaries.* He stood up slowly, stretching. *We might even pray together. Fanatical, that's what!*

It was barely three months since Tara had visited the Stephens family, but they were shocked at the change in her. Lank-haired and sullen, she shuffled across the room, stubbing her toes on the table leg as she sat down. She had not wanted to come; she never wanted to go anywhere these days. Her lips seemed to be glued together. It was only with tremendous effort, after a long silence, that she could bring herself to speak.

"Sometimes I sit in the room and I just want to cry and cry," she said. "No point in coming home at weekends. I've lost all my friends since I got glaucoma." She drooped in the chair. "I used to have a boyfriend," she explained to Ruth, "But not any more."

David moved uncomfortably in his seat, and avoided the pendeta's eyes. He felt bitter himself when he thought about Beni's suave retreat from that relationship — and yet, to be fair, had she ever really *had* his full affection? Beni was Beni, and always would be.

"What about Ani?" asked Jim. "You and she were always good friends, weren't you?"

"Oh, Ani!" Tara hunched her shoulders dismissively — unfairly because Ani had supported her through months of depression, coaxing her out when she shrank from meeting people, coming back again and again to the house in spite of some bitter rebuffs.

"It's a good place, the Blind School, though, isn't it?" asked Ruth. "We've been by it sometimes. Right at the end of the plantations, isn't it? Palm oil and rubber trees?"

"Almost in the country," said Jim. "Just the place for fresh air and cool breezes."

"It's depressing."

They waited for her to explain.

"They're nearly all blind there. Some of the teachers are too. And some of them have other things wrong as well." She shuddered. "Weird looking." But she knew it was not so much the other people that were repugnant as the thought that she too, one day, might be blind. Might? To all intents and purposes she was blind already. Desperately she clung to those hazy outlines, the jumble of colours and movement, and always she was haunted by fears of a dark future — shut in, black, unprotected — and utterly alone. "But old Ibu Tobing — and Pak Tobing too — they're the wardens — they have this way of talking to them. Just like they might talk to you. As if they liked them. As if ..." She waved her hands about irritably, "as if they were *people*!" She herself wanted to push them all as far away as possible. To label them firmly "Them" and not "Us". "And they're so *cheerful*, some of them! They'll tackle anything!" She thought of Elli, sitting on her bed each night, fingering her Braille Bible and singing. "There's this girl there, Elli. Looks horrible and can't see a thing. Must be thirty years old and no chance of ever getting married. But she's always smiling, always helping somebody. Keeps saying thank you to God for what He's done for her! I want to take her by the shoulders and give her a good shake. You stupid fool! I'd say. What have *you* got to thank Him for?"

She was getting quite agitated, and David looked at her in dismay.

"Elli sounds nice," he commented.

"Yes." Tara nodded. "You can't help but like her." She sighed. "Granny wants me to go back to the *dukun*."

"She would," muttered David.

"No," said Jim. "That's one thing you mustn't do."

"My friend at the hostel said, we know it's God who heals really, so it's all right if you pray to God first, and then go to the *dukun*."

"God won't be two-timed, Tara," said Jim solemnly. "You can't just mess around and play the flirt. In England we used to talk about black magic and white magic. I appreciate that there is a difference; but the root of it is all the same, and it's what you call it here in Indonesia: Powers of Darkness. They are not to be meddled with. You found that out with the saucer of ash. What happened to that, by the way? Have you still got it?"

"I didn't take it to the hostel. It's still lying around somewhere at home. But the ash is all gone, so it's quite harmless."

"Throw it away then. Don't leave it knocking around in the house."

"But it can't *do* anything, can it? Like you told us before, these things are only dumb bits of pottery that don't have any power. So why does it matter?" She felt a strong reluctance to get rid of the saucer; almost an emotional attachment to this thing she had so loathed and feared. "Well ... perhaps."

Jim knew that she would not destroy the saucer, and he was a little uncertain, himself, how important it was that she should. There was a danger of a sort of superstitious witch-hunt that saw evil spirits lurking everywhere and made out Satan's power to be greater than it was. And yet there was no doubting the reality of the spiritual warfare. He had watched as Indonesian Christians ministered in tiny village households, gently probing until one by one, from drawers and shelves and under floorboards, would be brought the half-forgotten tools of mischief. He had seen the freedom and the sudden release from fear and tension as they were solemnly burnt, and marked the change this could bring in family life and Christian witness. He sighed. They were so lacking in expertise in these areas; and as foreigners there was so much that they would never understand.

"You've got a Braille Bible now, haven't you — or is it the New Testament and Psalms?" She nodded. "Are you reading it?"

"Yes," she said, hoping he would not ask her which part she was reading.

"I think you would find the psalms very helpful. Some of them were written in times of trouble or depression just like you've been going through." He reached down a Bible from the shelf and turned to the Book of Psalms. "Like this one, see, Psalm 77." He began slowly to read through the psalm.

"I cry aloud to God; I cry aloud and he hears me.
In times of trouble I pray to the Lord;
all night long I lift my hands in prayer,
but I cannot find comfort ...
Will the Lord always reject us? ...
Has he stopped loving us? ...
I will remember your great deeds, Lord,
I will recall the wonders you did in the past.
I will think about all that you have done;
I will meditate on your mighty acts ..."

Jim looked across at Tara and smiled. "This man's really going through a tough time, isn't he, he's really down. But then he reminds himself of all that God has done, and so by the end of the psalm he feels confident that God is in control, and that He loves us and cares for us, even in the worst times."

"I sometimes think that if God heals me I'll be an evangelist."

Jim laughed. "Well, that's great, Tara. But you don't have to wait till then to start serving Him, you know. God can use you just as you are."

If God heals me ... She sighed. There would be

little point in it unless He healed her. She would have no good news to share.

CHAPTER ELEVEN

David was thinking a lot about healing these days. It was hard to avoid it, seeing Yesaya as he did almost every day.

"Why don't you come along to the Saturday Fellowship just one time?" Yesaya would urge. "Just to see what happens? You can't condemn a thing without even trying it, now can you?"

"I'm not condemning it," explained David. "It's only that – oh well, you know me, I'm an old conformist at heart. And you know what my father thinks about the prayer groups."

"Not only him," said Yesaya ruefully. "The elders would kick me out of the church, I expect, given half the chance. That's how much they care about faith! You only have to say 'Praise the Lord' and you're practically labelled a cultist! Suggest something new and they drop it like a lead balloon!"

Yesaya was smarting, David knew, because his proposals for the youth group to make evangelistic visits to the kampungs had been ignored by the church elders. He tightened his guitar strings a bit more and strummed a few chords before replying.

"They're a bottleneck, sure," he agreed. "But

we'll get there one day. Last Sunday was a start, wasn't it – just the two of us going off with Pak James?" Yesaya nodded grudgingly, and they both laughed, remembering the small half-finished church with its earth floor, and the two hens which would keep clucking around the back benches in the middle of the service. "Those kids were really keen, you know, at the afternoon meeting. We only need to get the whole team along one time and the thing'll really start to take off!"

"It wouldn't hurt to go along just once," said Yesaya, coming back relentlessly to the subject of the fellowship. "It's very, very good. I've told you that before. We get some tremendous speakers. First rate. The whole Bible comes alive and you suddenly realize it's true! True today, I mean. You'll see. We've been learning so much about faith. It'll revolutionize your whole thinking!"

"Mmm." That was what David was afraid of.

"And it's not just a spiritual fill-me-up. There's a practical, serving side to the fellowship. They send out teams, visiting around the hospitals, praying with people."

"Yes, I've heard about them." His Aunt Rini had been quite indignant, he remembered, when she was sick in the General Hospital. A crowd of students had marched in, she said, demanded to hear her sins confessed, commanded Almighty God in no uncertain tones to heal her, thrust a pamphlet into her confused hands with a curt order to "thank God she was well again", and swept out and on to the next cubicle. He grinned. It was probably the only time in her life that Aunt Rini had been at a loss for words.

"You'll come then," said Yesaya, mistaking the grin. "Praise the Lord!" He looked round hastily and put his fingers to his lips with exaggerated care. "Ssh! Beware of spies!"

It was easier, in the end, to go along with Yesaya than to keep on making excuses.

The fellowship met in a large house in a quiet part of town. The long front room had been made even longer by the removal of a partition, and the resulting hall was tightly packed. David and Yesaya were a little late arriving, and had to squeeze in at the end of a row near the back. David smiled apologetically as his neighbours moved up to make room, and was disappointed to receive only a polite nod when he introduced himself. He looked critically round the room; mostly young people, but a few middle-aged women near the front. He recognized some students from the Christian Union, but none from his faculty. Everyone seemed to be talking and laughing, but each cosy group was a separate unit – like a lot of raindrops which had somehow failed to become a puddle. Very different from his own church, where everyone knew everyone else, with all the back-biting, the boring sameness, and yet the sense of belonging which came with a community.

Yesaya was leaning forward to tap the shoulder of the man in front.

"This is Sukimin," he said. "He was very sick a few months back. But a team from the fellowship prayed for him."

"Yes, I was in the General Hospital," the man began eagerly, "I was lying there ..."

But the first chorus was announced then, and he turned back obediently to face the front.

With the choruses, and later the prayers and testimonies, came a merging together into oneness. David was no longer the objective spectator, evaluating the meeting; he was caught up into the atmosphere of praise and expectancy. The speaker, as Yesaya had promised, was powerful and carried conviction. David could not recall, afterwards, one word of his sermon, but he felt tremendously uplifted, and determined from now on to read his Bible more seriously, and to give more time to prayer.

The testimonies, however, he did remember, almost word for word. One tall, colourful girl, who described in great detail the visit of a small group to the nearby hospital, and the way they had prayed there for the sick. And Sukimin, whom they had met earlier. He was a wiry little man, slim-featured, with dark, glowing eyes.

"I was dying," he explained in a simple, straightforward tone of voice. "I had cholera and they rushed me into hospital, but it was far too late. Running at both ends and weak as a breath. I thought that was the end. As much as I was *able* to think, that is. And I was thinking what a mess I'd made of it all. And then these people came in." He nodded with his chin towards someone on the front row. "Never seen them before in my life. But they said did I want them to pray for me. I've never heard anyone pray like that. Strong! Powerful! And I got better." He paused. "My life's never been the same since then. I don't do the things I used to do – drinking and that. Rough stuff. No. I gave my life to Christ, and I want to tell everyone what Jesus has done for me!"

David was silent on the way home. Again and again, over the next few weeks, the question kept recurring in his mind. If God today answers prayer for healing, then what about Tara? Should he not be seeking this healing for his sister too?

Each Saturday, now, he went with Yesaya to the Fellowship. He had doubts about them still. They spoke so much, it seemed, about what God was doing for them – in terms of money, possessions and health – and not enough, he felt, of what they should do for God. But there was no denying their enthusiasm and commitment. David listened enthralled, week by week, as the tall girl, Lisa, recounted the experiences of the hospital visiting team. One day he wanted Tara to meet her. One day, he hoped, Tara would come along to the fellowship meeting and learn for herself what God was doing – and what might, perhaps be possible for her too. But she was so prickly these days, so prone to curl up in the bedroom, or on the back porch, refusing to come out and be seen.

Then one Saturday she seemed suddenly more approachable. Their parents were away, taking Granny back to the *kampung*, the smaller children were scrabbling about in the garden, and they had the house to themselves. Elvira had been asking questions about Braille, and Tara decided to give them a lesson, giggling delightedly each time they cheated, using eyes instead of fingers.

"Oh, it's no good!" said Vira before long, pushing the book away. "It's all too tiny! You need some extra nerves in your fingers or something!"

David ran the tips of his fingers across the page. With his eyes open he was beginning to memorize some of the letters. Six basic dots, and a wide variety of combinations; not too difficult as a code. But to feel, not see, the dots was another matter.

"I learned on a big board first, of course," explained Tara, "Putting nails in holes. That's much easier.

She was highly proficient now, punching the signs with a small tool and a grid placed over the paper. David was fascinated to watch her. It was disconcerting for a fully sighted person to see the lines of print on the old textbook which she was using as an exercise book. But he supposed that Tara was able to ignore them. He reached for the big Braille Bible with its plain white pages and the raised dots showing more clearly. It was a heavy, unwieldy book, and he wondered if she would be bold enough to take it along to the Saturday Fellowship sometime.

"You say the chapter and verse, and I'll find it," she offered.

He watched her turning the pages and wondered whether this might be the moment to mention the meetings. Suddenly she found the verse, John 3:16, and began to read, her fingers fluently tracing the words.

"For God so loved the world that .."

"Here's Yesaya's Honda!" called Elvira from her seat by the window. "Ani's with him ... Oh – and a car ... There's two other people come with them in a car."

Tara snapped the Bible shut and felt round for her belongings, ready to flee to the bedroom. Not people. And especially not strangers. Not here. Not now. But David caught her wrist and pulled her gently towards the front door.

"Hello, come in! Lovely to see you." He recognized Lisa and the *pendeta* who often spoke at the Saturday Fellowship. His throat felt suddenly very dry.

"Sit down. Sit down."

Vira melted smoothly away, returning presently with glasses of tea and banana crisps in a bowl. Tara suffered the introductions, murmuring a shy "Good afternoon" in not quite the right direction, and reaching out a tentative hand which was grasped in a strong firm one. Tara's sight was hazy now, but there was no mistaking the decisiveness of the *pendeta*. Tall, assured, he stood and sat with the air of taking the world squarely and finding it very good. Lisa was tall too, queenly in her movements, with skilfully applied makeup and a sophisticated hairstyle.

"You've been visiting at the hospital," said David. It was a statement, not a question.

"Yes," said Ani, smoothing back her wind-ruffled hair. "We've been round the military hospital."

"We've been ministering to the patients," said Yesaya. "Some of them are so sad looking, you know. You should come with us some time, David. We shared the Word of God, and we prayed with them, so that Satan would be bound in their lives. You could really sense the Lord at work. Really! Some of those faces were radiant as we came away!" His eyes shone. "It's such a thrill, and a privilege, you know, to feel that the Lord can use us to help these people who are so sick."

"And now we've come here," said Lisa, "To minister to you."

"To us?"

"To Mutiara."

Tara looked up quickly. "To me? To pray for me to be healed, you mean?" Time stopped; the click of a camera shutter, and they were all immortalized, immobile, in her memory.

Ani nodded. "That's right, Tara dear."

"Yes, er, oh .. That's great," said David, rather

taken aback, in spite of having longed for just such a thing. "I was just about to bring the subject up, actually ... So we could talk it over a bit, you know. Ask the Lord to show us His will."

"You want to be healed, don't you, Mutiara?" asked the *pendeta*.

She nodded. Her blouse felt tight, and it was suddenly very difficult to breathe.

"Do you know the Lord is speaking to you today, this minute?"

"He is?"

David swallowed. He felt a need to put out a hand and somehow slow down the whole process, and he didn't know quite why. Ani caught his eye and smiled. "Don't worry," she mouthed. "Only trust the Lord and relax."

The *pendeta* was speaking slowly and solemnly to Tara, emphasizing each word. "Do you believe that Jesus is able to save you from sin and deliver you from all sickness?"

"Yes."

"Do you reject the Powers of Darkness – *kuasa gelap*[1]? Have you any magic charms or tokens? You must throw them away."

"Yes ... er ... No."

"I do not accept this illness, Mutiara. We will cast it out in the name of Jesus."

He rose, and she dropped to her knees as he placed his hands on her head. Lisa and Yesaya,

---

[1] Lit "powers of darkness", used of the occult.

Ani, then David and finally Vira, gathered round. The *pendeta's* voice was deep, and he prayed with power, authoritatively, commanding the spirit of blindness to leave this child of God, and exhorting the heavenly Father to defeat evil in her life and restore her sight. David felt breathless. Was this the best thing they had ever done? Or the worst? Panic, apprehension, dread, hope — and a sudden resurgence of faith as he mentally reached out to grasp the strong hands of Jesus, lifting him above the waves.

Tara trembled as a broken-winged sparrow might, when held in friendly, yet alien, hands. A thousand thoughts fluttered round in her mind. *Yes Lord, heal me, please make me see again.* How heavy his hands felt, how compelling his voice, how long his prayer. *I'll do anything*, she promised, *only make me well — make me happy — let me have friends again — and get married — and be normal*!

"... In the name of Jesus Christ our Lord and Saviour, Amen!"

The hands were lifted and Tara slowly, cautiously, opened her eyes. Would it be straight away clear, diamond sharp — or fuzzy at first, blurry? David felt his whole body tense.

"Now you must thank God for healing you," said the *pendeta* sharply.

Oh yes. She remembered hearing somewhere that you had to say "thank you" first to make it happen. "Thank you, Lord for healing me." She blinked.

"Praise the Lord! Oh how wonderful!" Yesaya was beaming as he helped her to her feet.

She stumbled as she sat back — almost fell back, on the settee, looking round at the expectant, questioning faces.

"You may not feel too different straight away," murmured Lisa, "But you need to praise God and thank Him that He has already heard and answered our prayers, and you are already healed."

Everything seemed blurred. But not as blurred, surely, as before? More like trees walking, perhaps. She remembered that was how it happened in the Bible.

"How do you feel, Tara?" David searched his sister's face for signs of change.

"Do you see, Tara?"

"Can you see me, Tara," said Vira from away by the door.

"Yes ... yes ... I think it's a little clearer .." then less hesitantly, "Yes, thank you, God! I *do* see better!"

Ani hugged her and they left, Yesaya singing loudly as he revved up his motor bike. "Praise the name of Jesus! Praise the name of Jesus!"

The *pendeta* enclosed her hand in another firm handshake. "Praise God, Mutiara! Keep away from evil powers; and praise the Lord." He turned to David. "Are you coming to the meeting tonight? You could all three come along, and Mutiara can give her testimony."

Tara made a small gesture of protest.

"I think not, not tonight, Pak," said David. "Better to leave it a little while."

The minister nodded, Lisa flashed them a charming smile, and they went off in the blue Toyota.

CHAPTER TWELVE

"The Lord has done something wonderful last night," said Yesaya as they bounced along in Pendeta James' jeep the next morning. "David's sister has been healed! The one who was going blind!"

"Mutiara?" Jim glanced up to catch David's eye in the driving mirror. "That's wonderful news, David! How did it happen? Can she see now like she did before?"

"Yes."

"It was last night."

"Well, er ... "

Everyone started speaking at once. David cleared his throat and began again. "Well, the pendeta from the Saturday Fellowship came round with ... "

"Oh, they have a pendeta, do they? I hadn't realized it was that formal." Almost like a church, thought Jim. No wonder the church leaders don't like it. "The prayer groups don't usually have ordained pendetas, do they?"

"Well — I suppose he's a pendeta."

"He was in a Pentecostal Church before, I think," said Ani. "But he's only one of the people who speak at the meetings. There's a committee who actually run the fellowship."

"And he prayed for Mutiara at last night's meeting?"

"No, at the house. Yesaya and Ani brought him round, with a girl called Lisa."

"She's got a gift of healing," explained Yesaya. "She goes round the hospitals praying for people."

"The pendeta laid hands on her and prayed. You should have heard his prayer!"

"And she was healed? She can see again?"

"Yes," said Ani and Yesaya together.

"Well," said David, "It's a bit hard to tell, actually."

"Oh, David!" Yesaya protested. "Her face was radiant! She was almost in tears, she was so overcome with joy!"

"You see, it was quite difficult before, to tell how much she was seeing," explained David. "She didn't want people to know, you see, and she'd be acting as if she could see all right, and then she'd stumble, or do something really stupid — or she'd put a hand out and start getting nervous, and you'd suddenly realize she could hardly see a thing. Her eyes are open, you see. And they don't look any different now."

"She *said* she could see better," said Ani thoughtfully. "But it doesn't always seem to begin straight away, just like that, does it? Even when Jesus healed that blind man, he saw men like trees walking, at first, and then Jesus did something else before he could see properly."

"In Mark's Gospel, you mean?" said Jim. "It's true there were two steps there, but it was all really one occasion. There were other times, like Blind Bartimaeus, when Jesus healed completely in one stage."

"I'd hate to think I was *preventing* her from being healed," said David with a worried frown, "By not having enough faith."

"Oh, I don't think you could do that," said Jim.

"I thought she'd be coming along with us today?" said Yesaya.

"Oh well, she doesn't sing in the group, does she? And she has to get back to the hostel this afternoon," David explained. "All the same ... Well, she seemed a bit on the verge of tears this morning ... You know, she's *saying* she's better, but it's almost as if she's trying to convince herself."

"I suppose they told her that she must praise God and thank Him *before* she sees the results of the prayer, did they?" suggested Jim. "And that was how she would show her faith?"

"Did they? I don't know. Yes — I suppose it was something a bit like that."

"It's true, though, isn't it?" said Yesaya. "I've read lots of books like that. The person thanks God because He's already answered their prayer — and it's only then that they are healed."

"Well, it's true that we can thank God because we know He has heard our prayer, and we believe He is already answering it; He promises in His word to answer our prayers. And sometimes it can be as we claim the promises that we see them coming true. But it's not a magic formula that we recite — any more than God is like the old idols — perform the right ritual and you get what you want. God is our heavenly Father, if we've come to Him through Jesus, and we tell Him our deepest needs and concerns, just as we ... well, perhaps you *don't* tell your fathers things?" They all laughed and shook their heads. "But we can tell our heavenly Father everything, because we know that He loves us *and* understands us, through and through. And because He loves and understands us we can trust Him to be working in the best possible way for our good."

"So you don't think Tara's been healed?"

"Oh, I didn't say that! I hope when we get back we'll find that she's not gone back to the Blind School because she doesn't need to. I believe that God can and does heal people through prayer. But if we find that He *hasn't* healed Tara, it would be quite wrong to say that He has, wouldn't it?"

David sighed. It all sounded right, but it was not really what he wanted to hear.

CHAPTER THIRTEEN

"How's Mutiara?" Jim asked Pak Sitompul when they met in the church the following Sunday morning.

"The same," said Pak Sitompul. He disliked being questioned about the family. "Got another appointment at the eye hospital tomorrow," he added.

"Oh yes?"

"They give her a new prescription for the eye-drops. And then there's new glasses every so often. She takes the eye-drops every day and still she needs stronger glasses!" He grunted. "Always more expense!"

Jim nodded thoughtfully as he opened his briefcase and shook out the folds of his gown. It was not, perhaps, the right moment to mention prayers for healing.

Ruth was still unloading the children from the car.

"Now boys, what do we do in church?"

"Stay quiet," said Mark obediently.

"That's right. We sit quietly during the service, and then we come out and shake hands and say good morning – *Selamat pagi* – to all the people."

Mark wriggled protestingly and he shook his head. "Don't want to."

"Otherwise, people will feel very sad if you are unfriendly and don't shake hands with them."

She slammed the car door shut, and turned to smile across at Mutiara and her mother, who were just coming in through the gate.

Ibu Sitompul was a good guide, sensitive to Tara's need but unobtrusive in her instructions, keeping up a low commentary as they walked along.

"Here comes old Ibu Hartono, she's been very sick lately, they wondered if she would pull through ... Good morning Bu, how are you feeling now? Bit better, are you? ... And there's Samuel's wife with their new baby, what a sweet little thing ... Hi there, sweet girl! Are you feeding her yourself? Good, good ... and here we are at the gate ... and there's the missionary's wife. Pendeta James Stephens must be preaching here today. Good Morning, Bu."

"Good morning, Ibu Sitompul. Hello, Mutiara, how are you?"

"Good morning." Mutiara smiled noncommittally. Was she walking more confidently, Ruth wondered, with a firmer step? Or was that wishful thinking? Her eyes looked big as usual behind the dark glasses.

Mark was jumping up and down, eager for once to say hello, and Tara shook his hand with a solemn smile.

"Good morning, Mark, Good morning, Daniel."

Daniel giggled as he took her hand for a moment, then trotted off after his brother.

Two or three women with babies stood chatting together by the church steps, and round the side, under the giant palm tree, Tara could tell that a crowd of young people were laughing together as they leaned against their motorbikes. There was a sudden roar, and a flash of red and black shot in through the gate to join the rest. Tara could not see how many there were there – just a buzzing mass of colour and movement – but her ears were attuned, by now, to the voices of those she knew. Very clearly across the general hum she could distinguish what Vira was saying.

"Oh yes, they were all there, laying hands on her and praying. A proper prayer meeting. That handsome pendeta – you know, the one from the Saturday Fellowship. He prayed for her ... Nothing happened though."

"Oh, *poor* Tara, she must be *so* disappointed."

Tara had not heard that voice for quite some time, but instinctively she recognized its purring quality for Rita's.

Her mother was still talking to Ibu James. "We're taking Mutiara to the eye hospital tomorrow," she explained. "She has an appointment there every three or four months now."

"Ssh ... here she comes now."

"What a shame ..."

Tara ignored the voices, her face set and expressionless, but her grip tightened on her mother's arm as they strolled – oh so slowly – towards the church. She felt a sharp dig in the leg, and a small hand thrust itself into hers.

"Are you my friend, Tara?" asked an anxious voice.

"Yes, Mark, I'll be your friend." She tried for a smile, but all her mental energy was straining towards the group under the palm tree.

"Up the steps now," murmured Ibu Sitompul. They left the missionary family with the nursing mothers on the back row, and moved slowly towards the front. "There," said Ibu Sitompul as she settled herself in the pew and began searching in her bag for her hymn book. "We'll see very nicely from here."

Tara did not bother to disillusion her. Even from the foremost pew, she knew that the church elders and the English pendeta would be indistinguishable against the solid brown expanse of the pulpit area.

As the congregation filed past at the close of the service, Jim had time enough to ask Mutiara to call round at the house later and see them. She looked doubtful; coming to church had been ordeal enough, and all she longed for now was to go home and sink into oblivion. But Jim caught David too, at the end of the line, and pressed him to bring her.

"She's very depressed I think, isn't she, and she

could do with talking it through a bit – don't you agree?"

David nodded. He was feeling like someone with third degree burns himself; all raw, hurting flesh which could not bear handling, and he did not want to ask too much of himself.

But it was a relief, in some ways, to talk about what had happened. The subject was never mentioned at home. They had told Ibu Sitompul, a little, but no one had dared to reveal to their father that some of the hated Saturday Fellowship had had the effrontery to pray in his own front room.

"Not that we were to blame, exactly," explained David. "We hadn't asked them to come. But there's no sense in getting him upset for no reason." He paused. "If it had worked, of course, we'd have told him straight away ..." His voice trailed off and he stared gloomily into mid-air.

"Why didn't it work?" For the first time Tara voiced the question she had asked herself a hundred times. "Did I not have enough faith? I *thought* I believed – it seemed as if the very thing I'd been longing for was going to come true."

"Yesaya reckons it's my fault, I think," said David, "Because I was so doubtful about it all in the jeep last Sunday."

"How much faith do you have to have?"

Jim smiled gently at Tara. "Well, the Bible tells us that we need only as much as a grain of mustard seed, Tara, the tiniest of seeds," he said. "The founder of our Mission put it another way. He said it's not having great faith that counts, but faith in a great God. And that's it, isn't it. Not how much we believe, but Who we believe in."

"Is it? I do believe in God – and Jesus."

"Jesus couldn't do miracles in Nazareth because of their unbelief," said David.

"That's what I heard Yesaya telling you this morning, isn't it?" Jim pushed his chair back with a gesture of annoyance. "That Fellowship! I do not think it's helpful to go around practically blaming people if they're not healed! We hear so much ..."

"Jim ..." Ruth caught his eye and he shrugged his shoulders.

"Oh, yes. Yes. All right."

"You don't like the Fellowship, then?" asked David.

"Oh, I wouldn't put it that way, David. I'm tremendously impressed by some of what they do. Some of their teaching – and their witnessing – is really good. But I don't care for this whirlwind ministry – in, pray, out – not enough real counselling or pastoral follow-up."

"Do you believe in healing, though?"

James hesitated a moment before answering. "I believe that God can heal people – in many ways. The body's own natural defence system, for instance, which He designed. That's an amazing healing mechanism which God uses. He heals through medicine and the work of doctors. And I believe that God can heal people in extraordinary, miraculous ways – and sometimes He does."

"But?"

He laughed. "No! No 'but'. It's only that it's a controversial subject, and I don't claim to have all the answers. We're learning all the time. Take that village we went to last week. You remember the old man where we ate after the service? They had some in that kampung who were very sick a while back. Tried everything – *dukuns* couldn't help them. In the end even the *dukun* told them to go to that old man so that he could pray for them. And they got better! He prayed for them to be healed and they are healed. The Lord used that to bring three whole families through from animism to Christianity."

"There you are!" said Tara bitterly. "Everyone gets healed except me!"

"Oh, Tara!" Ruth's heart was aching as she looked across at her, wondering what she could possibly say that might bring comfort.

"I'm sorry, Mutiara," Jim said. "You wanted God to heal you, just like that – and He didn't. We don't know why He didn't do that. Though it may be that He is in the process of healing you; maybe your appointment at the hospital tomorrow is part of that process. But we don't know that. But prayer isn't a spell, you know, that either works or it doesn't work. Prayer is all about a relationship; and relationships are more complex than that." He glanced at David, who nodded in agreement. "Jesus promises that we can ask *anything*, if we ask it in His name. That's if we are really seeking His will. But we can't *demand*; we can't manipulate God, or try to bargain with Him. Not usually, anyway. He wants to be Lord in our lives, not a slave." He paused. "And sometimes He seems to do that by taking the props away, until we see what's the most important thing."

Tara sat, her eyes downcast, hands resting in her lap.

"God sometimes sees it differently from us. Like the man who was paralyzed in my sermon this morning. The four friends wanted him to be able to walk. But Jesus went straight to his deepest need and said 'Your sins are forgiven'."

But he did make him walk again, thought Tara.

"You know that Jesus told a story about you, don't you?"

"About me?" She looked up, then.

"About your name: Mutiara: the pearl. You know it: the man who found the perfect pearl. It was so beautiful, so valuable, and he wanted it so much, that he had to sell everything else that he had in order to buy the pearl without price." He smiled as he asked her softly, "What would be *your* pearl, Mutiara? Your eyesight is important, I know, but that's not what Jesus meant by the pearl. Sometimes we need to spend time sorting out our priorities first; 'Seek ye first the Kingdom of heaven', you know the chorus, 'and all these things will be added unto you.' "

Mutiara rode home on the back of David's bicycle. Her mind felt wooden. In the end she nudged him to stop, and they dismounted and walked the last part of the way.

"Is he saying that if I repent, then God will heal me?" she asked. "Because I'm not sure that I really want to." She thought back to the Pentecostal pendeta asking do you repent, do you believe, do you reject black magic – and she had answered automatically as expected. But was it true? Did she really want that costly pearl? Was it worth it? She wanted God to step down and heal her; then get back to heaven, where He belonged. She wasn't planning on some sort of a takeover.

David made no answer. He felt sure that God ought to heal if she repented. But to repent in order to be healed sounded not quite right.

Pendeta James had completely failed to explain, in any convincing way, why Tara had not been healed. But they prayed together before leaving, and it had been not the formal, verbose prayer of his father, or the strong, assertive prayer of the Saturday Fellowship, but a simple voicing of their confusion, and a sense of leaving the subject in more capable hands. Suddenly David had realized why Pak James kept talking about being God's children. Flashing into his mind came the long-forgotten picture of his mother's tiny clock, swept off the cupboard in some mad whirl and crashing to the floor. He must have been six or seven at the time. He remembered the way his heart had stopped; and how his father had bent down and scooped up the fragile treasure. "Don't worry," he had murmured as he carried it away to be mended. "She'll never know." David had never before, and rarely since, felt so close to the dark, brooding presence that was his father.

CHAPTER FOURTEEN

The hospital buildings were as drab and as dreary as ever; the waiting patients as doleful; even the ducks pecking about near the hedge seemed to droop. Mutiara's name was called, and she endured the dispassionate examination of Dr. Sinaga; the light flashing, the fingers pressed on her eyes, the reading tests which by now seemed a mockery. The minutes lengthened as the doctor sat, frowning abstractedly, the prescription pad ready in one hand and his chin resting in the other. Was it time for stronger glasses, Tara wondered. She could see Dr. Sinaga quite well, just the other side of the desk, but the bustling nurse was constantly swinging in and out of focus as she moved about at the edge of Tara's range of vision. Tara was reminded of one of those mosquitoes that buzz round so close – then dart off as you are about to swipe.

"I think we should operate," the doctor said eventually, looking across at Ibu Sitompul.

"Oh!" Tara gave a gasp, and the cold, thoughtful eyes turned her way. "You must understand that this will not restore your sight. What is destroyed is already dead, and can't be saved. We will ease the pressure. This will stop the pain, and we hope it will prevent you from going blind."

An operation! She was falling down a deep shaft, falling endlessly. The ground fell away beneath her feet. The whole world flashed by. Still she fell. An operation. What had Pak James said? Usually God heals through doctors and medicine.

An operation. "How much would it cost?" asked Ibu Sitompul.

"An operation?" said Yesaya, when he heard. "But she's been healed! She's had hands laid on her, and we all prayed – and we've been praising God for healing her!"

"Yes, but ..."

"She doesn't want an operation, David! God is healing her!"

"But she can't see any better than she could before we prayed," said David, "And the doctor seems to think she'll end up completely blind if we don't do something drastic."

Yesaya dumped his music on top of the organ and sat down heavily on the stool. "That's what faith is all about, David!" he said earnestly. "Believing that God is at work. In spite of all the evidence to the contrary. Believing He's answered our prayers."

"But maybe He's answering them through this operation?"

"Oh no, no, no!" He began thumping out the chords of a rousing chorus. David sighed. "We'll keep praying for her," Yesaya added. "That's what she needs – not some gloomy dump of a hospital!"

"It's not *your* sister," muttered David, "You might not sound so sure if it were." But he knew he was being unfair. Yesaya was one of their most faithful friends, and no one could accuse him of not caring.

"An operation?" said Ruth. "And does the doctor say that will make you better?"

"He says it won't mend what has been destroyed. But it will get rid of the pain in my eye and it will stop me from going completely blind."

"Oh well, that's something, Tara."

"But I went to the Saturday Fellowship last night and ..."

"Yes?"

"Well ... They say I shouldn't have the operation. They say we should pray. And thank God for healing me. That's all."

Ruth gave her a searching look. "We've all been praying for you, Tara. But I think if the doctor advises you to have surgery, then you should, don't you?"

Tara nodded slowly. "I guess so."

The operation was scheduled for the evening of March 4. Mutiara was instructed to check in at the hospital the day before.

"Oh no," muttered Pak Sitompul suspiciously. "They'll not catch us out that way! Extra day's fees for nothing! You'll go in on the day and not before."

It was already dusk when they arrived; Mutiara, her mother and grandmother and Elvira, in two *becaks*. Ibu Sitompul had decided, at the last minute, that they should eat first, at home, to save carrying rice and everything with them into the hospital, where no food was provided.

"You won't want it later, anyway, Tara," she had said. "Not after an operation."

She did not want it now, either; her insides were a fluttering mass of seasick butterflies. But she knew that her mother would be fussed enough, bringing meals in over the next few days, so she meekly accepted a plate of rice and toyed with it abstractedly while her feet tapped the floor in nervous impatience. It had seemed an age before David was sent out to summon *becaks* and she was gathering up her bag and saying goodbye.

A row of handcarts had been set up by the hospital entrance, selling noodles, fried rice, nuts and cigarettes., It was visiting time; a throng of people were coming away as they approached, laden with baskets and cans that bore the remains of the patients' suppers.

Ibu Sitompul led the way to the office to check in.

"Mutiara Sitompul? We expected her yesterday." The voice was cold and forbidding. "I'll check with Dr. Sinaga."

Tara wilted under the strong air of disapproval

as they were led along the covered path to the wards. One door tightly closed; an elderly man looking vacantly out from the next; from the third doorway came the murmur of voices, hushed as they entered. Brown walls, brown floor, brown beds, some denuded of mattresses and showing only the bare brown wooden boards. On the near left-hand side one a woman lay back against high pillows. Thick bandages covered her eyes, and she moaned softly as her hands worked endlessly at a red woollen shawl. Beyond her a much older woman sat crosslegged on the empty boards, a little pile of bags and belongings at her side, watching. Granny and Elvira would take it in turns to attend Tara in the same way; to give food and daily care as needed, and to call for help in an emergency. Tara put her things in the cupboard, hanging her towel over the rail. The nurse was explaining at great length about the preparation needed before surgery, and the absolute necessity of coming into hospital 24 hours beforehand. *Maybe they'll put it off until tomorrow now*, thought Tara, and her heart lifted.

But they didn't.

Dr. Sinaga was coldly furious.

"You realize that we have had no opportunity to monitor you during the day," he said, scribbling away at his green cards. "I shall operate, nevertheless, at the appointed time."

Mutiara was sitting up in bed when Ruth Stephens called at the hospital the next day. Thick white bandages covered her eyes, but she recognized the missionary by the brisk tap-tap of her feet across the floor.

"Hello, Mutiara, how was it?"

"Terrible!" Tara shuddered. "I thought I was dying!" She grimaced, remembering. "They thought so too!" She waved her hands across the ward to where an old woman lay sleeping. "I screamed so!"

"Cried all night," added Granny, nodding solemnly as she chewed at her betelnut.

"And I was oh so sick to my stomach! All the rice I'd eaten came back!"

Ruth was horrified. "But whatever were they thinking of, to let you eat rice before an operation?"

"Oh well ..." said Tara vaguely. It was all over now. Already she was beginning to feel excited; to feel impatient for the moment when the bandages would come off.

"How long must you wait?" asked Ruth, but she could give no answer. A week? Ten days? Dr. Sinaga never volunteered information, and that she should be brave enough to ask was unthinkable.

"Shall we pray together?" Ruth suggested.

She read first, part of Psalm 40, and Tara followed with her fingers in the Braille Bible.

"I am weak and poor, O Lord, but you have not forgotten me.

You are my Saviour and my God – hurry to my aid!"

"Weak and poor," repeated Tara. "That's me all right. But God will come to help me, and I shall see again."

Ruth looked at her in concern. Tara seemed to be expecting a miracle. That was not, surely, how the doctor had put it?

Weak and poor, thought Tara, as she listened to the retreating footsteps, *but you have not forgotten me.*

She hugged the thought to her during the following week; feeding on the assurances of Ani and Yesaya when they came; ignoring the cynical comments of Vira and the dark mutterings of her grandmother; pushing aside the cautious qualifications of the missionaries.

One question was uppermost: when will they remove the bandages? Each day the doctor came and went, without comment, and she dared not ask. Then finally, unbidden, the answer came.

"Tomorrow we will remove the bandages."

She could hardly wait.

CHAPTER FIFTEEN

"We'll take the right eye first, and I want you to look straight ahead."

The doctor's voice was a dry monotone, but his fingers felt firm and comforting on her face as they worked to remove the bandage. The background hum of conversation was hushed; the air heavy with suspense. Tara felt hot, sticky, tense, her whole being concentrated on a tiny spot behind her eyes.

The ward was dimmer than she had expected, but even so the light hurt her eyes; a shimmering fuzz, like heavy rain obscuring a windowpane. She stared straight ahead as the fuzz cleared, straining to distinguish shapes in the hazy brown distance.

"Do you see the nurse?"

She peered into the gloom. A white blur appeared from one side and came closer. Tara nodded slowly as the nurse took form by the bed.

"Now the other eye."

The nurse was tense too, Tara could see now. Her hand gripped the bars of the bed and she was leaning forward, gazing fixedly at Tara as if willing her to see.

"Yes, I see you fine," said Tara, and the nurse's shoulders sagged visibly as she relaxed. Suddenly everyone was talking, as if the volume had been switched on again.

The brief awareness of the nurse as a person, as someone who cared, was unnerving, and Tara's eyes flooded with hot tears which spilled over to run down her cheeks. She would not acknowledge any other reason for them; nor for the choking feeling in her throat or the tightness in her chest. Dr. Sinaga droned on, but she scarcely heard him. Eventually he stood up to go, taking his entourage with him. Tara waited till they were out of earshot before flinging herself back on the pillow and giving rein to the heaving sobs which racked her body.

"There you are, it's worth it in the end, isn't it? It's worth all the pain, just so you can see again."

The voice came from across the ward; the wavering singsong of the old woman who had had cataracts removed. Tara had heard her yesterday, telling everyone how wonderful it was; she would be going home later today. Tara made no answer. She considered sitting up on the bed, turning round, looking across at the old woman and smiling at her. But she knew that it would be quite, quite pointless. She could see neither more nor less than she had done before. The old woman was too far away.

Ruth went with the pendeta's wife, Ibu Saragih, to visit the Sitompuls. They had called first at the hospital, and been told that Mutiara had already left. Tara could hear them explaining as she lay in bed in the next room.

"We thought she would be kept in another day or so after the bandages came off," said Ibu James.

"No need," grunted Pak Sitompul. "Cost enough as it is! The operation failed," he added.

"Oh dear, can't she see, then?"

"It failed?"

"Yes, it failed, She's no better now than she was." He shook his head. "They don't know what they're doing, these doctors! They've made a mistake." He stabbed the air accusingly. "They've made a mistake and we ought to complain, by rights! They've done it wrong, and she's no better than she was!"

Ruth exchanged glances with Ibu Saragih. What could they say? They turned in relief to Mutiara's mother, coming through from the kitchen with a tray of cold drinks.

"So the operation was unsuccessful?" said Ibu Saragih.

Ibu Sitompul sighed as she put down the tray and sat down. Her anxious birdlike face was creased with worry. "Tara's maybe a little better," she said. "She seems to see a bit more with one eye than with the other. And the pain has gone."

"Oh yes," said the pendeta's wife, "I remember she had bad headaches."

"Well," said Ruth, "That's *something* to be thankful for, isn't it — if one eye is reasonable!"

In her bedroom Tara snorted and turned over to face the wall.

"How does she feel about it?" asked Ruth. "Is she very disappointed?"

"She's very upset," said David, coming in through the front door in time to hear the question. "Of course she's disappointed. We all are." He nodded to the two visitors and came over to join them. "Yes, she's disappointed," he said again as they shook hands.

"She's sleeping now, I think," said Ibu Sitompul, nodding a signal to Vira, who shuffled across to the bedroom door. She had the grace to go in and close the door behind her instead of calling from the doorway. Tara hunched her shoulders and stared fixedly at the wall as she approached.

"You've got *two* pendeta's wives to see you," Vira said in a harsh whisper, "Our own church one and the English one! Nothing but the best for Mutiara!"

Tara ignored her. She was trying to remember the name of that king they had learned about years ago in Sunday school, the one with the wicked wife — Jezebel, wasn't it? And Ahab was the king. He had wanted a field, a vineyard, and he couldn't have it, so he went to bed and turned his face to the wall. At the time Tara had thought he was childish to sulk so; but now she could sympathize.

"Come on, Ra!" Vira shook her roughly. "We know you're awake!" She waited a moment but there was no response. "Oh! Be like that then!" Vira turned away crossly and stalked out, slamming the door behind her. "She's got to face up to reality some time," Tara could hear her exclaiming, "She's going blind and that's that, and it's not going to change so it's time she got used to it!"

"Oh, but Vira!" Their mother's voice was gentle, reproachful.

"Well, it's natural she's feeling depressed just now."

"It's very sad at her age."

"Have a bit of sympathy, can't you, Vira!"

Everyone spoke at once. Tara sighed and rolled over, feeling with her feet for the rubber thongs under the bed. Wearily she pulled herself up. Fortunately the bathroom opened directly from the bedroom, so she could splash cold water on her face and tidy her hair a little before going out to face her first visitors since the operation.

The two women were very solicitous; their pity was almost tangible as they fumbled with pious platitudes that might — but woefully failed to – give comfort.

"You don't have any pain, though, now?" asked Ruth after an awkward silence.

"No. No pain," admitted Tara.

"I'm not sure how far you can actually see?"

"Three metres."

Three metres! That seems quite a lot, thought Ruth, *considering she stumbles so much. But perhaps that's the outside limit, and what she clearly sees is much less.*

"That's with your glasses on?"

Tara nodded. "My good eye."

"Did the specialist say that the operation had failed?" probed Ruth.

"No."

"Well, he wouldn't, would he?" put in Ibu Sitompul. "They don't admit it!"

Ruth nodded thoughtfully. She was wondering if it was really the operation which had been unsuccessful, or the family's false expectations which had failed to materialize. "Eye operations are very difficult, I think, because the eye is so delicate. A mistake could easily blind the patient instead of curing him." She paused. "But as I understood it, the doctor did not actually promise to reverse the glaucoma, did he?" The words sounded odd in Indonesian, and she tried again. "I mean, he said he could not make you better, Mutiara — only prevent it from getting worse."

"You mean, she'll never get better?" said Ibu Sitompul in dismay.

"But she might have gone completely blind," said Ruth earnestly. "We can praise God that the doctor has managed to stop that! And to ease the pain, too."

Praise God. Tara's face was expressionless as she looked across at the missionary. *We read all these Bible verses telling us how Jesus heals the sick, and God helps the poor and weak. We have a pendeta laying hands on me and who knows how many people praying for me. And now I should praise God because I don't have headaches and I'm only half blind. What a blessing!*

CHAPTER SIXTEEN

David saw the visitors out to the car.

"Do you know what Tara did with that saucer of ash?" Ruth asked him.

He looked at her blankly.

"The thing she got from the *dukun*. Did she throw it away?"

"Oh yes, there was something." He thought for a minute. "I don't know. Could that be why she's not been healed?"

"Not necessarily, David. You may have to accept the fact that her vision will always be very poor. But it's wrong and it's dangerous to cling on to those spirit things."

David lingered by the gate, watching a fat old duck waddle down to the edge of the ditch and lean precariously forward to poke with her bill at an empty cigarette packet. Strange that Yesaya should have been talking about *dukuns* and magic only the day before. He had been very dogmatic about the dangers of occult involvement, insisting that charms or tokens could be a block to healing. David had dismissed the idea. "Oh, we don't get mixed up in that sort of thing," he had said. But that was not quite true. At the back of a drawer was a little charm that his grandmother had given him when he started at university — no, before then, when he was still at high school — a talisman to aid the memory and give power in study. He could not have refused it without causing hurt and offence, but of course he did not believe in it. Or, at least ... He wore it whenever he sat an exam. Presumably the two older girls had been given charms too, by now, to help them pass exams. David bolted the latch and went quickly inside. He found them in the kitchen.

"Tara," he began, "What did you do with that ash?"

"The saucer from the *dukun*?" she answered warily. "The ash is gone long since, but the saucer ... is still around somewhere." She paused. "Do you think it matters?"

"Well ... Ibu James seemed to think so. And Yesaya's been giving me a lecture about spirit things."

Tara was silent for a moment. "To be honest I'd like to get rid of it," she said at last, "But I was scared. I didn't know what to do with it. I pushed it away at the back of the cupboard."

"Let's talk about it after the meeting tonight," said David decisively. "You'll come to the Saturday Fellowship, won't you, both of you? There's sure to be someone there we can talk to about it."

"I didn't really want to go," said Tara slowly. "I didn't want to go anywhere. But yes, all right then."

"And you, Vira?"

"What, that Fellowship?" Vira sounded scornful. "No thank you. They don't seem too successful with their praying where Tara's concerned, do they? No – I've got better things to do on a Saturday night, thank you!"

David was not surprised when the subject of the meeting was announced as *Kuasa Gelap*: Powers of Darkness. It all seemed part of the pattern. The speaker was an ex-*dukun* who had come to know the Lord, renounced all the trappings of witchcraft, and eventually gone on to seminary in the United States. His ministry now was directed towards freeing people from involvement with evil spirits; and he was urgent on the subject in season and out of season.

"My people have exchanged me," he read from Jeremiah,

"The God who has brought them honour,
 for gods who can do nothing for them ...
On every high hill and under every green tree
 you worshipped fertility gods."

"On every high hill," he repeated. "Our whole society is riddled with spirit worship. Is it any wonder the churches don't grow, and the Christians are divided among themselves? Worthless spirits, God calls them! That old grandmother didn't know very much when she was alive, did she? So is she suddenly wise now she's dead? Why do you asked her advice then? Why do you listen when she speaks in a strange language in someone's throat at an *adat* ceremony? And what will you do on Easter Saturday? Won't be long now. Will you spend the night in the graveyard, eating and drinking? Will you make a little hole, and pour drinks down, so that Grandfather can join in the festival? Don't!" He brought his fist down on the table with a thud. "What did the angels say to those women when they came at first light to the tomb on Resurrection Day? They said, 'Why do you seek the living among the dead?' Don't do it! He's not there any more! If he was a Christian he's with Jesus now — he doesn't need your old fruit syrup! And if he wasn't he can't harm you." He shook his head. "We don't need to fear the spirits of our ancestors. God's Holy Spirit can protect us from all harm."

He paused for a moment, to look steadily around the room, as if assessing his audience one by one. "What about *jimats*[1]?" he said softly. He held up his arm so that they could see the veins in his wrist. "How many of you have been to the *dukun* and had a piece of metal inserted here, in your arm?" He raised his voice as he repeated the question. "Have you had something put in here to give you power over your mother-in-law? Power over that boss at work? We all like power, don't we? And how many are wearing charms round their necks to protect them on the roads, or to get them through exams?"

---

[1] Magic charm or token, giving protection from evil spirits.

David fingered the little charm in his pocket. He was determined, now, to get rid of it.

"Are you a *Christian* asking *evil* spirits to protect you? The Lord Jesus gives us victory over all the spirits! And he doesn't need charms to do it with!" He paused. "He only needs your trust." He seemed to be looking straight at David, and then at Tara, as he added, "Every charm, every tool, every magic ritual gives Satan a foothold in your body. No wonder you get sick or have nightmares. You've invited Satan in and he won't go till you throw him out, baggage too!"

After the meeting David and Tara joined the group who were seeking ministry in a side room. Each had brought something to be destroyed or thrown away; charms, bracelets, love potions. Tara took the old saucer from her bag and smashed it on the hard tiled floor. Then after a moment's pause, she threw down a silver bracelet on top of it. David tossed his charm with the others on the pile. The ex-*dukun* prayed with them as they deliberately renounced any involvement with evil spirits, spending a few moments with each one to think through what further magic objects might be hidden away at home, what past experiences might need to be confessed. David was silent. There were many things, he realized, that had spirit connotations; strange figures over some of the doors, odd bits of ritual to be performed at some of the big family occasions. He had never inquired too closely into their meaning, and it was not for him now to go dismantling the ornaments at home. That must come from his parents. But he felt cleansed now, washed clean through and through. It was the most conscious act of commitment that he had yet made. It seemed as if he had set his feet firmly on a path that was good; and from which there would be no turning back.

"There's a story in the Bible," said the preacher, "Perhaps you know it, of a spirit who was cast out of a person. He roamed the countryside, looking for a home, and eventually he went back and found that same person like an empty house, swept clean and waiting. So he brought seven other spirits and they all moved in. And the person was worse off than before." He looked solemnly round the group before continuing. "You have chosen to clear out your houses this evening, each one of you. You are ready to receive a guest. The Lord Jesus stands at the door and knocks. Will you let him in? He is waiting to do just that." He paused, then added emphatically, "Beware of an empty house!"

There was much to think about on the way home.

"Yes, I do want you in my life, Lord," David was saying under his breath. "You've been here a long time now, I know, but I think perhaps I've been keeping you out in the front room, and filling the back rooms with a whole lot of junk. I want you to take over the whole house, Lord. It's all yours. I want to serve You."

CHAPTER SIXTEEN 125

It's always a little bit more, Tara was thinking. *All I want is to be healed. But they always seem to be asking something more of me. And still I don't see!* She sighed. He had been much more exciting to listen to, but really this man's basic message had been the same as the pendeta in their own church, and the same as the missionary pendeta. At least the *dukun* in the kampung had only wanted money! But she dismissed that thought instantly. She knew that the way of the spirits was wrong; and dangerous. There was no going back along that path. But should she go *forward*, along the Jesus path?

Their parents were watching television when they got home. Pak Sitompul shot them a dark look, muttering something under his breath about the prayer fellowships. Ibu Sitompul looked round in surprise.

"Isn't Vira with you?" she asked. "I thought she was going with you to the Saturday Fellowship?"

"No, she didn't want to come." Tara shrugged and went throught to the kitchen for a plateful of rice. "Want something to eat, David?"

"Mmm. Yes please." He sat down in front of the television. The Late Night News was just starting.

"Well, where *is* Vira then?" Ibu Sitompul frowned anxiously. There were far too many things to worry about these days.

The News was nearly over when they heard a motorbike roar to a halt outside. Pak Sitompul sprang up and flung open the door, ready to give a piece of his mind to whoever was bringing his daughter home at such a late hour.

A young boy stood on the path. He was breathing heavily, irregularly, and he was trembling.

"There's been an accident," he began.

Ibu Sitompul felt her insides turn over. David set down his plate and rushed over to the door.

"Why, it's Beni's brother!" he said in amazement. "What are you doing here?"

"Come in," said Pak Sitompul heavily.

"It's Beni," said the boy, hovering just inside the doorway and twisting his key ring round and round as he shifted from one foot to the other. "He was on the Honda. Just coming out on to the main road — and a great jeep came hurtling down — smashed straight into them!" He gulped. "Caught them bang on the side!" He slammed one fist into the other palm to demonstrate. "Thrown off the bike. Vira too ... She was on the back!"

There was a gasp from Tara as it suddenly dawned on her why this boy was here. "Vira ... Beni ..." Her hands gripped the arms of the chair.

"The bike's all smashed up ... They've taken them to hospital ... General Hospital ... Beni's not too badly hurt they think — may have a bone broken ... Vira ... Vira ..." He faltered. "Vira's unconscious ... Coma," he added softly.

Ibu Sitompul groaned. Her legs folded under her as she sank down on to a chair. Pak Sitompul stood stock still, like a statue enduring one more heavy downpour. Woodenly he repeated the facts. "An accident ... Vira ... In a coma. The General Hospital."

"But Beni's in Jakarta!" protested David. Nothing seemed to be making sense any more.

"No. He came home for my sister's wedding. Been home two or three weeks now — staying till after Easter ... Thought you knew ... They were going to a party."

Tara closed her eyes. Beni. Beni and Vira ... *Vira*! ... How *could* she!

CHAPTER SEVENTEEN

It was seven o'clock on Sunday morning when David rang the missionaries' doorbell. Ibu Stephens peeped through the curtains, then flung them wide open. David watched as she slid back bolts and unlocked the door.

"My sister is dead," he said.

"Dead!" Ruth motioned him inside and they shook hands mechanically and sat down.

"My sister, Elvira, is dead."

"Elvira!" Ruth gaped at him, open mouthed. "But ... how? ... When?"

"A road accident." He was ashen-faced. The knuckles shone as his hands gripped the arms of the chair. "She was thrown off the back of a motorbike."

"Oh dear." Ruth sat dumbly, her hands in her lap, her eyes big and wet as she looked at David's haggard face. "I'm so very sorry, David," she said, inadequately, in English. "I'll get Pak."

Jim was towelling himself dry after a hasty shower.

"It's David," whispered Ruth, "His sister has died."

"Mutiara?" said Jim, astounded.

"No. Elvira."

"*Elvira*!" He stared at his wife for a moment — then turned to open the wardrobe door, rifling through the hangers at top speed to find his black clerical shirt. "Elvira," he repeated, at a loss.

"She's been killed in a road accident."

David sat back, eyes closed, as he waited. He had been up all night and his head was throbbing. Telescoped before him was the hospital bed with its white sheets, its tubes and instruments, its battered, still figure, and all around the family sitting, hollow-eyed, despondent.

He looked up at the touch of the pendeta's hand on his shoulder.

"David, I'm sorry. What a shock for you all." Jim took David's arm as they shook hands, feeling the tension in his body. He was much paler than a brown-skinned Batak ought to be. "What happened?"

"It was a crash."

"Last night?"

"Yes." David stared at the floor for a moment. "You remember Beni?" Jim nodded. "He's been away, in Java, but he's back now, for a while ... Beni took Vira out on his Honda. They were going to a party or something ... They had an accident ... A jeep ran into them." He paused, reliving the events of the night. "We'd just got back from the Fellowship when they came for us. I couldn't believe it! They were in hospital, both of them ... Beni's hurt, of course, but not badly. Lots of bandages — broken leg and bruises. We saw him. Fairly straightforward break." He shook his head. "Making a fuss ... I don't think he realizes about Vira ... He didn't seem too clear about anything, much ..."

Beni had been loud in his complaints, giving orders left and right to his attentive relatives. But he seemed to have no idea how he came to be in hospital, and he had never once asked after Vira.

"And Vira?"

David swallowed, hard. "She was smashed up — thrown right off and hit the ground ... and the jeep ..." His voice trailed off.

"She was sitting sidesaddle?"

"Yes. She looked terrible." He shuddered. "She was in a coma ... we stayed all night. Pendeta Saragih came ... There was never any hope ... She died about half an hour ago."

"In God's mercy," said Jim gently. "Thank you for coming to tell us, David."

"I'm on my way now, to let everyone know. They're bringing her home this morning ... You'll come?"

"Yes, we'll come." He nodded slowly, considering. "I'll follow you back now, David. I've a couple of services later this morning, out of town, but I'll come round and see your parents for a while first. And we can both come this afternoon — can't we?" He glanced across at Ruth, who nodded. "And we'll certainly be praying for you. We'll pray together now, shall we?"

There was no mistaking the house. A red flag marked the road, and a huge canopy had been stretched out over the yard. Aunt Rini's army had been at work since sunrise; clearing the big front room of furniture and laying down straw matting; borrowing chairs for the yard and glasses for the guests. Family members would come from miles around, and Aunt Rini lost no time in organizing a team of helpers to cook for them. Mutiara chopped onions, red-eyed, till her back and her arms ached. The carpenter and his lads came early and set up trestles outside the back door. Soon came the rhythmic sawing and wood shavings began to fly.

Elvira's body was brought home as soon as the formalities were completed and bills paid. She lay at first on a mattress in the centre of the front room, but by midday they were able to transfer her to the new-made open coffin. An elaborate wreath of purple orchids stood as a headboard against the wall. Ibu Sitompul, a skeletal figure in black, with dark shadows round her eyes and tear streaks on her cheeks, leant back against the wall at one side. Her husband sat crosslegged on the mat at the other side of the coffin. His face was ravaged, his eyes bleak and staring. Neither had slept.

All day people came; neighbours, relatives, friends. Some simply greeted the couple, shaking hands in silence and pausing for a moment by the coffin before they left. Others stayed on, sitting in groups on the floor, men one side and women the other, carefully covering their legs and feet with *sarungs*. Still more sat about on chairs in the yard, gossiping, or nodding solemnly as they chewed betelnut or smoked.

David was waiting by the gate when the church group arrived; the two pendetas with their wives, three church elders and their wives, Yesaya, Tomo and some others from the youth group, all spilling out from three cars. An uncle and aunt arrived at the same time and came wailing dramatically up the path, in the traditional manner, bursting into noisy tears as they stepped through the door. About fifty pairs of shoes lay jumbled by the step. The church people added theirs to the pile and followed the wailers inside.

Aunt Rini nudged Tara to stop working, and the cooks rinsed their hands under the kitchen tap before going through to join the mourners. Ani took Tara's hand and they knelt together by the coffin. Granny was there too, acting out some ritual in a moaning, tearful Batak chant; now bending down to touch Vira's face, now stretching her arms wide, now clasping her hands together as if in prayer. She seemed to be speaking exclusively to the figure in the coffin; for no one in the room was paying the slightest attention to her gestures.

Everyone seemed subdued by the dark, sombre room. Through the open window came the low tones of a mournful dirge. There were to be ten ceremonies, as representatives of various groups, from school, work, neighbourhood, each paid their respects with a short speech, and if they were Christians with a hymn and a prayer. The church would be last, with the proper funeral.

"Let's sing out, shall we?" said Pendeta Saragih as they waited their turn, "So that we may support the family as the Christian Church."

"We'll drown them out," murmured Yesaya under his breath.

The pendeta announced a hymn number. No one had hymn books. Following the usual practice he read out each line of the verse before they sang it. They made quite a crowd, altogether, and their strong, Batak voices rang out rich and deep. The Christians crowded round the open doorway to swell the congregation; but most of the crowd in the garden continued their conversation without a break, ignoring, it would seem, the funeral service.

The pendeta read briefly from Revelation: "... He will wipe away all tears from their eyes. There will be no more death, no crying or pain. The old things have disappeared." Then he turned back to Thessalonians. "We do not need to be sad," he began, "as are those without hope. Paul says here, and we also believe, that 'Jesus died and rose again, and so we believe, that God will take back with Jesus those who have died believing in him.' This is our hope," he explained, "as Christians ..."

Ruth listened carefully, straining to distinguish the Indonesian words through the buzzing of background noises. She wondered what hope

Elvira had known. They had never really got close to her. Too busy with Tara, perhaps, when the two girls came to the house. Elvira had been merely the companion, the one who teased the children, or sat silent — apart from the odd cynical comment. Not the one they had tried to draw out or felt concerned about or prayed for. And now it was too late.

Jim thought how simply and clearly the pendeta was speaking; a message of comfort for the family and a plain expression of the Gospel in a few words for the benefit of the non-Christians around them. He glanced across at Ibu Sitompul's taut, grey face. She looked utterly bereft, and completely exhausted after her sleepless night. He was glad that the *adat* rituals, with their links with paganism, had been kept to a minimum.

Mutiara was remembering all the times when Vira had made spiteful remarks about Beni. "Superman" she had called him, in that mocking voice. But even then there were hints, perhaps — hindsight added colour to the details — little signs that she had wanted him for herself. *And to think I was jealous of Rita! And Vira was there — waiting her chance!* Tara wondered how her sister had known that Beni was home. Had she written to him? How had they met? Not a word to anyone. And to sneak off to a party with him! As the others bent to pray, Tara knelt up by the coffin to look down at the figure lying so still there, her hands clasped together on her chest. She wanted to hate

Vira; bitterness choked her like a weed; almost her mouth formed the words, "You cheated. Now *that's* your fate!" But at the sight of death she drew back. Shock, grief, pity, loss; all were there; and a deep sense of guilt because she knew that the resentment was there too, like a stubborn weed. However much she said to herself, "Vira was my sister. I loved her," still that bitter root remained.

David was turning over and over in his mind an imaginery scene of what he should have said to Vira and how she might have replied. How he could have encouraged her to go to the Christian meetings after school, or the church youth group, or to read her Bible at home. How he might have shared his growing faith. He remembered what Pendeta James Stephens had said to Tara that night about the pearl of great price. That was the basic question, he realized. Where did you invest your money, your talents, your time, your very self? On something eternal? Or fritter them away? What had Vira thought about it all? He had never really taken her seriously — she was just his little sister. Now he would never know. He glanced at Tara, kneeling by the coffin. What's *your* pearl, Tara? he thought.

Tara did not distinguish David in the brown-grey crowd, but her thoughts turned suddenly to that evening when the missionary had asked her, "What's your pearl?" What's the most valuable thing of all? With a shock she realized that not once, since the news came of the accident, not once had she envied Vira. Many times, during the depressions of the past years, she had said, and had believed, that she wished she were dead. Now in the face of death she was very, very glad to be alive — even partially blind — even totally blind if it should come to that. There was more to life even than sight. For the first time she looked squarely into a future which might include blindness, and she determined to fight — if not for sight then at least for a life worth living. She would work hard at that school. She would try for a place at that college in Jakarta. She would train to be a teacher. If it had to be a blind teacher, so be it.

The pendeta was announcing a hymn, and there were sounds of scuffling as the lid of the coffin was brought in through the doorway. Following the *adat* ritual, Granny threw up her hands and wailed in Batak, "Why did you have to leave us? Oh why did you have to leave us?" The air was heavy with the sense of a young life cut off too soon. Then the singing began, and the first nail was hammered home in the coffin. The dam burst and Tara wept.

Much later, at the graveyard, Tara suddenly found herself standing next to the missionary's wife. The funeral was over; people were beginning to drift back to their cars. On an impulse, Tara caught Ruth's arm and drew her to one side.

"Ibu James," she began tentatively, "Supposing that in August, I was able to go to college. There's a college in Jakarta — where I could train as a teacher I mean, to teach blind children."

"Oh yes, Tara, that would be wonderful," said Ruth.

"Do you think there might be a grant, from Europe?"

"Oh well," Ruth hesitated. "I'm not sure about that, Tara. But we could try to find out. Our Mission doesn't really reckon to give financial aid ... But there might be something through the Dutch Church ... the mother church of this one, that is." She folded her *sarung* and stuffed it in her bag. "We'll talk about it later, shall we?" She squeezed Tara's arm sympathetically. "We're very, very sorry about Elvira," she added.

"Yes." *Yes*, she thought, *I am sorry, Vira. Please God, You get rid of the bitterness, because I can't do it.*

David was talking to Pendeta James by his car.

"What happened about those teams that were suggested, to visit the *kampungs*?"

"Evangelistic teams, you mean? We had a committee meeting about that the other day. We're hoping that each church will provide a team which can visit the villages in their area. I'll be helping to coordinate them. Are you interested?"

"Yes. Very."

"We'll probably be starting training sessions next month. About four sessions first, then we start the visiting programme. We'll go to those places where people have asked for Christian teaching." His eyes shone. "It's exciting, isn't it.

To see how many places there are like that, which are so open to the Gospel right now!"

David beckoned to Yesaya. "You want to join the team, don't you?"

"The evangelistic team, is it?" said Yesaya. "Yes, I do."

"Good! You need to see Pendeta Saragih first, to get your names on his list. Then we try to coordinate the various churches to fix dates for the course. It's quite a commitment, timewise, you realize? Training sessions first, then the visiting, with feedback sessions in between *kampung* visits. Think you can cope?"

"Of course," said Yesaya. "No problem. It's all for God's glory, isn't it?"

David nodded more slowly. "Yes, it will take time. But I want to *give* time. I want to serve the Lord." He paused, looking back towards the grave and his parents, still standing there. "All this with Elvira — well — it sort of gets me *here*, you know." He patted his chest. "I feel I must be *doing* something. Something to spread the Gospel!"

"I know," said Jim. "Makes you aware of the realities, doesn't it? But you don't need to feel guilty, David. That does happen sometimes, when someone dies. Along with the shock and the grief — and the anger, perhaps, against God. A sense of regret — all the things you should have said or done — or wished you hadn't done or said. But we just have to bring that to the Lord, for His forgiveness — and leave it there."

They piled into the cars and drove away. The family came last, drained and numb; carried along, as if in a dream, by the accepted patterns of behaviour. Pak Sitompul sat rigid; isolated, in his grief, even from his wife who shared it. She leaned back with her eyes closed, and let her sorrow sweep over her. But for David, and perhaps too for Mutiara, it was as if, somehow, a tiny glimmer of light was just beginning, oh so faintly, to appear at the end of the long, dark tunnel.

CHAPTER EIGHTEEN

The road was scarred and pitted. Some of the holes had been hastily filled in with rough stones which jutted out to add to the bumps. The jeep jolted along, shaking its passengers like dried beans in a can.

"Not much further," said Jim. "It's just this one really bad patch, and then we're on to the smooth again."

They were in second gear now, edging cautiously down a rock-strewn slope that resembled a dried-up river bed, with high sandy banks on either side. Then at the bottom they rounded a bend and emerged on an open expanse of paddy. The headlights picked out the deep ruts of tyre tracks leading smooth and straight ahead of them across the middle of the rice fields. Darkness smothered them like a blanket, pressing in on the top and sides of the car. Then they were at the other side, rounding another bend and climbing. They could see lights; one or two at first, glinting through the trees, then gradually more and more. Oil lamps, large and small, shining from the wooden houses that lined the road; well spaced at first, each with its surround of hard, bare-swept earth, then closer and closer packed. They swung round a last corner and bumped to a halt beside the open square at the heart of the *kampung*.

The evangelistic team tumbled stiffly out and stood easing the feeling back into their cramped limbs.

"Here's my uncle," said Pak Sembiring, and they all turned to greet the old man, who ushered them into his little *warung*[1] with a wave of the hand and a toothless grin.

"How's the leg, Pak?" asked Jim.

"Better, better. Look!" He held out a foot which had been badly burned some weeks back, when a lamp had been knocked over. "Much better, now, see!"

His wife shook their hands and bustled about pouring glasses of coffee. David and Yesaya began tuning their guitars as the others took their seats round the table. A crowd of ragged children gathered to watch.

"Are you singing Jesus songs?" asked one of the boys, gapetoothed, in a torn shirt, with a carved horn charm hung round his neck.

"You want to hear our songs?" asked Yesaya. "Come on, then."

He led the way on to the square, and the children sat round in a semicircle as he strummed a few opening chords. Ani came over to lead the singing.

---

[1] Food stall or simple café.

"Orang Kristen yang menang tepuk tangan,
Kar'na sudah ditebus, tepuk tangan ...

Christian people who are winning clap your hands,

If your sins have been forgiven, clap your hands,
Look at all the joys above,
Full of glory, full of love,

If you're happy and you know it, clap your hands."

"Now you try," said Ani, smiling round at the crowd which was growing steadily larger. "You clap when I clap. See?"

"Orang Kristen yang menang ..."

Shyly at first, but with mounting enthusiasm, the children joined in the chorus, and the next one, and the next. Ibu Sembiring stepped forward, with her posters, to tell them a story. The lamps hissed and flared, but the children were hushed now, as she talked.

"Here is the pool where all the animals of the jungle liked to come, every day, to drink the water. It was cool, clear, clean — and oh so delicious to quench their thirst! But one day, when they came to drink, what did they find?" Deftly, she flicked the paper over to show the next picture. "What was it?"

"A wall!"

"A great, high wall." She stretched her arms wide. "It was so long — they couldn't see the end of it. So high — couldn't see over it — couldn't see through it. How could they reach that beautiful pool with the cool, clear water? What could they do? ... Well, ..."

In the *warung* the team members sipped their coffee as the other tables gradually filled. It was nine o'clock. The work in the fields was done, the sweat-soaked workers bathed and rested, the evening meal cooked or reheated and eaten. People were beginning to congregate, on porches or in *warungs*. More and more children, of all ages, were coming out to join their friends on the grass. Small girls swayed to and fro, on the fringes, rocking smaller babies slung in cloth slings from their shoulders. Old women sat on verandahs and in doorways round the square, chewing betelnut, heads nodding as they gossipped and listened to the story. The men were collecting in the *warungs*, talking, drinking coffee, smoking, gambling, one eye on the television and the other on the entertainment in the square. As Jim stepped out with his Bible in his hand and began to read, some of them moved nearer to join the congregation proper.

"There are many things that people are afraid of, aren't there?" he said. "Afraid of sickness, of bad harvest, afraid of enemies, afraid of the spirits. So many things people have to do because they're afraid of the spirit's anger if they don't do them. But the God we believe in is stronger than all the spirits, and He tells us that perfect love casts out fear. Hear what Jesus said about the way God loves us.

'For God so loved the world, that He gave His only Son, that whosoever believes in Him should not perish, but have everlasting life.'

Amazing, isn't it? As we were singing in that last chorus; God's love is so high, and so deep and so wide ..."

The missionary spoke in Indonesian, and Pak Sembiring translated his words, phrase by phrase, into Karo Batak. Sembiring was the sales manager of a pharmaceutical firm. He had a good job with a high salary, and a well-kept house in one of the better parts of Medan. He had paid very few visits, since qualifying, to his home *kampung*. But a few months back, attending a big family funeral, he had learned that a group in the village had heard the Gospel and were eager to receive Christian teaching and to start a church there. Fired with enthusiasm, he was ready to invest heavily from his own pocket to give financial backing to the building project. After being a Christian for many years, and a church elder for two, he had suddenly realized that yes, the Gospel is Good News, and he was very keen to share it.

"Have you any questions?" he asked at the close of the meeting. "There must be many things you would like to know more about?"

"What does it mean?" asked one of the older men. "What would it actually mean if we become Christians? Do we have to give up our powers?"

"Magic powers?" asked Pak Sembiring.

"Healing powers. Do we have to stop healing people?" added the man, frowning.

"Do you pray to the spirits when you heal people? Do you use *mantras*, or rituals, like sprinkling flower water?" The man nodded slowly. "God says we can't worship Him *and* the spirits. We have to choose," said Pak Sembiring. "It's one or the other." He paused. "But you could still use herbs and spices for healing — like rubbing ground ginger on those aching bones. That sort of *kampung* medicine is good, and it's cheap."

"But how do you tell which is which?" whispered Yesaya. "Better get rid of the lot."

The old man drew out a small *kris*, special dagger-sword with its deadly wavy blade. "This is what I use," he explained. "No spirits, no *mantras*. Not any more. Now I pray to the Christian God to heal the person. I point this *kris* up towards the sun and I say some words."

"What words?" asked Jim, in Indonesian.

"Oh — any words. It doesn't matter."

"You believe in Jesus now?" asked Jim. "You want to be baptized?" He nodded. "Jesus, you know, has more power than any spiritual forces. If God wants you still to heal people, could you simple pray for them, in the name of Jesus? Without using the *kris*?" The man looked doubtful. "Because if not, you are trusting the *kris* to heal people, aren't you — not Jesus?"

"What happens when we are baptized?" said another voice.

"Do Christians eat pork? And what about dogmeat?"

"Could you help us to repair our waterpump?"

"He wants to get rid of that *kris*," Yesaya whispered to David. "He knows what he should do, and they're dithering instead of pressing him to a decision. Doesn't Pak James realize the *kris* is magic?"

"May I borrow?" One of the *kampung* boys reached for David's guitar and began softly strumming. He was humming one of the choruses over to himself.

"Tinggi, tiada yang lebih tinggi,
Dalam, tiada yang lebih dalam, ...

So high, you can't get over it,
So deep, can't get under it,
So wide, ..."

"It's true, you know," David told him, "Jesus' love really is higher and deeper and wider than anything else."

"Yes, I know," said the boy, his eyes sparkling. "I don't get scared any more, in the dark. Ever since you started coming here, I just sing one of these songs and I know that God can protect me against the spirits. Even the dead can't harm us."

"Do you want to join the catechism classes, when we start them, and be baptized?"

"Yes, I do."

David and Yesaya smiled at each other in the lamplight.

"How was the *kampung* visit?" asked Ruth, when David called at the house a few days later with Tara.

"It was good. Very good!" David grinned. "Some of those folk are so keen to learn! So many questions!"

"They are, aren't they?" agreed Jim. "It's thrilling to see them thinking it all through. You see the need, now, for the training sessions."

"Yes," said David. "I've been thinking a lot about training lately." He paused, wondering how to continue, and Jim turned to Tara.

"Are you all set, Tara?" he asked. "How do you feel about it all?"

Tara was due to leave the following week for Jakarta. She had a government scholarship for the College for the Handicapped there, and a bursary from the Dutch church which should cover most of her additional expenses. With the promise of a teaching post at the blind school in Medan on completion of the two-year course, Mutiara's future seemed assured.

"It's not certain yet, of course," she explained, "I have to take an entrance exam when I get to Jakarta."

"Oh — that's nothing!" Ruth brushed it aside with a flick of the hand. "They would never send for you to go all that way if it wasn't a certainty. The test will be just a formality, I'm sure! After all, they have the report from your teachers here!"

"How will you get there, Tara?" asked Jim. "Can someone meet you at the other end?"

"My aunt is going with me," said Tara. "She has to go to Jakarta anyway, on business. I can travel with her, and I can stay at another uncle's house in Jakarta until I can go into the hostel."

"Oh that's good," said Ruth. Tara's sight was very poor now, and they had been wondering how she would cope with all the technical details of flying. She was more open, now, about her disability, and easier to help — and they were more aware, consequently, of just how limited her vision had become.

"It's a Muslim family," she added. "But they don't mind if I go to church."

"We can give you some addresses too," said Jim, springing up. "We have Christian friends there who would be only too glad to welcome you, I'm sure." He disappeared into his study and returned a few minutes later with a piece of paper. "Here are the addresses, see. This is a missionary couple, and these are Javanese Christians who used to live in Medan. We'll write and tell them you're coming. And this is our mission office. You could always ask for help there if you needed to."

"I'll ask Mrs. Smith to call at the hostel if she can," said Ruth. "But don't be too shy to visit them, will you? You could take a friend. Tell you what," she added with sudden inspiration. "I'll give you a little something you could take them, if you would — a little gift from us."

CHAPTER EIGHTEEN

"Thank you." Tara smiled. "I'll try."

"The pendeta gave you a letter of introduction to a church there, didn't he?" asked Jim. She nodded.

"We'll be praying for you, Tara," said Ruth, "Especially for Christian friends in the hostel. You'll soon settle in."

Tara smiled at them. "It's like new hope. So much less than I wanted. But this is what I've got, and I'm going to make something of it."

"Good girl. We'll be at the airport to see you off."

CHAPTER NINETEEN

The Sitompuls reached the airport well ahead of time; Mutiara's parents in their best clothes, Granny in her dark *kain* and *kebaya*[1], and all six surviving children. The two smaller girls wore frilly pink dresses, and sat demurely and selfconsciously on the edge of their seats. Tara stood with David by the window, waiting for Aunt Rini, who was always prompt to time, neither early nor late.

"I hope she won't be too bossy," murmured David.

"I don't mind. I'll be glad to be organized on the plane," said Tara, who was very nervous about the journey. She could feel herself trembling inside, but no one seemed to notice. "I'm sorry for Edi."

David laughed. "Well, he's asked for trouble — and he'll get it!"

Aunt Rini was going to Jakarta to deal with a son who had supposedly been studying at university there. It had suddenly come to light that he had never, in fact, begun the course, but had spent the

---

[1]Traditional dress of women — long-sleeved blouse (kebaya) worn with a piece of material (kain) wrapped round to make a long skirt.

past two years living wildly on the money his family had provided for his education.

"Have you got those addresses the missionaries gave you?" added David.

Tara nodded. "They're in my bags somewhere." She pressed her forehead against the dark tinted windowpane. "I don't know if I'll use them, though."

"Oh but Tara, why ever not? It's worth making contact," said David. "You may be glad of their help some day. And it would be useful to help you get started at a church there."

"You think so?" She looked at him steadily with her big, dark, near-sightless eyes. "I don't know. It's not been much use to me so far." She waited for him to speak, then as he stood, dumbly, she added, "Nor the *dukun* either." She shrugged. "Or the doctors. There's nothing been much use."

David looked back at her, shocked into silence. He felt the hurt, the dejection, he understood the disillusionment. But he was so convinced now, in his own experience, of God's love, that he could not doubt God's care for Tara too, in spite of everything. Yet how to express that faith? Easy to say, "God loves you" when it was she, not he, who was virtually blind.

"Oh well," Tara sighed. "If I'm very lonely I might call and see them."

"I'll pray for you, Tara." That at least he could say. "Every day."

"Thank you. Yes, thank you David. Thanks a

lot." She turned away to look out of the window. "Remember that meeting we went to? The night of Vira's accident?"

"I remember."

"Do you remember what he said about Jesus, standing at the door and knocking?"

"Yes?"

"Well ..." She paused. "I feel like I'm there, inside, and I'm standing right by the door, with my hand on the handle. Only I can't decide ... I'd *like* him in, in a way — even though he's not made me see again as I asked. It's just that ... I don't know whether to open the door or bolt the latch hard!" She laughed, awkwardly. "I don't mind going to church now and then — but I don't know that I want him taking over my whole life — not like he's taking over your life!"

"It's worth it though," said David gently. "Here's Aunt Rini coming now, and the Stephens family too — and Ani — and Yesaya. And here comes Rudi, your friend from the blind school."

Aunt Rini reached them first, bearing down imperiously with her husband and children flanked on either side. "Are you checked in yet, baggage checked? Not too much cabin baggage?" She looked at her watch. "Five minutes more, then we go through. No sense in dawdling."

Everyone was crowding round. Tara's head swam with the jumble of lights and faces and sounds.

"God bless you, Tara," said Ruth.

"Don't forget to visit our friends in Jakarta," added Jim.

"Tara!" Ani hugged her tight. "You'll write, won't you?"

"Goodbye, Tara," said Rudi. "We'll keep in touch, won't we?"

The goodbyes seemed endless. The two English children were quite carried away by the excitement, and rushed around shaking hands with everyone.

"*Selamat jalan*! Have a good journey! *Selamat jalan*!"

"Come, Tara!" said Aunt Rini, and she led the way through to the departure lounge.

The family made their way to the waving gallery. Mark and Daniel scrambled up the long flight of steps like mountain kids, and raced along the wide corridor.

"Quick! Quick! See the planes!"

Jim and David took the two boys to the far end of the gallery, where they could watch a plane refuelling.

"There's one, Mark! Just coming into land now! See the lights!"

"Mandala, Mandala! It's got propellers!" yelled Mark. "Boom! Boom!"

They watched as the plane swooped down to land, and moved off gracefully to the far end of the runway.

"I've appreciated having you on that evangelism team, David," said Jim. "It makes a big difference having the group there to open things up with the singing."

"The children always love to sing."

"And I think you have a gift, too, for sharing your faith with others."

"Do you, Pak James?" David screwed up his eyes against the sun's glare, as he watched the plane turn slowly round and begin to creep lazily back towards them. "I've been wondering if maybe ... Well, actually, I feel quite sure ... that I should do some theological training. That God might be calling me to serve Him in the church."

Jim looked at him sharply as they turned to walk down the gallery. He had been thrilled to watch David's faith growing over the past few years, and he longed for just such faithful, committed Christians to take up the challenge of full time ministry. But it would not be easy.

"Have you mentioned this to your father?" he asked. "You'll finish your engineering course first. I presume? You've still two years to go, haven't you?"

"Well, it should be. Yes, I'll finish that first, I hope."

"Good." Jim nodded slowly. "I'm quite sure that God wants to use you, David, and He may well want to use you in the ordained ministry. But it's good to have this year or two first, to test the call. How does your father feel about it? Have you told him?"

"A little." David grimaced. "He was angry. I

was taken aback! I mean," he closed his eyes, remembering the scene. "He's a church elder, and we've always gone to church and Sunday school and all that. I thought he would be pleased!"

"But he wasn't?"

"Furious!"

Pak Sitompul had sat in silence for a long few moments, then groaned, head in hands. "First we have a little boy takes a fever and dies. Then a daughter starts going blind. Then another daughter gets herself killed. Now my eldest son wants to throw away a good education and fine career prospects to become a church pendeta!" He sighed. "What is all this? Has someone put a curse on me or something?"

"It's understandable," said Jim. "After all, engineering is a top profession here in Indonesia, and everyone thinks that theological colleges are full of people who couldn't get in anywhere else. And too often, that's true! But he'll come round, given time. He takes his eldership very seriously, you know. We'll pray for him — and for you too."

"Here they come now!" called Ani. There was a rush to the front of the waving gallery as the passengers surged out below them, and began to walk across the tarmac to the waiting plane. Not this one, nor these ... not them ... They walked in driblets; singly, then a couple, then a group, each with an air of purposeful haste. Eventually they saw them unmistakeably; the faltering, hesitant girl urged on by the brusque, well-built woman.

Ruth gave a little gasp as Tara stumbled and slipped at the kerb.

"Her aunt is not such a good guide as you, Ibu."

"Oh, I *do* hope she'll be all right," said Ibu Sitompul. "So far away! Even if she could see I'd worry. But as it is ... she seems so vulnerable!"

"I know. But she has to go, doesn't she?" said Ruth. "It's such a good opportunity. We have to let go — give her into the Lord's keeping and trust Him to watch over her."

Aunt Rini turned, at the foot of the steps, and they all waved frantically, conscious that Tara, of course, could not see them. She looked small and lost, dwarfed in the distance against the huge plane, as she gave a half-hearted, bewildered-looking wave, and turned to climb the steps to the plane.

Her footsteps echoed with a metallic ring, ominous to her ears. But a smiling stewardess was waiting just inside the door, to guide her smoothly to her seat.

"Good to have a window seat, as you've not flown before," said Aunt Rini, tactlessly.

Tara silently examined her seatbelt and fastened it, first try, with an impressive clonk. The cool air, red plush seats, and the noise of bustle and movement all around were exhilarating. She giggled; excitement trembling on the brink of hysteria.

"Plenty of people to see us off, anyway," commented Aunt Rini. "Who was that blind boy?

One of the Blind School students? Good thing I got you into that place. Nice of the English *pendeta* to come — and what was in that envelope Ibu Stephens gave you?"

Tara slit open the envelope; some money and a card. The plane was already moving as she handed it to her aunt to read out for her.

"Don't be afraid or discouraged, for I, the Lord your God, am with you, *wherever you go*. Joshua 1:9."

Tara took back the card without speaking and tucked it away. *Wherever you go.* She braced herself, feeling the thrust of the engines as the plane thundered down the runway and took off into the future.

David watched the great white and red bird rising majestically into the clear blue sky.

"Goodbye, Tara. God bless you. *Selamat jalan.*"

POSTSCRIPT

Well ... There it is. She's gone now. Not the ending we'd hoped for, perhaps. We wanted it all cut and dried before she left, a success story for the Stephens' prayer letters. But this is what Christian work so often is, isn't it — the world over. One sows, another reaps. You try to teach and lead, you give advice or just an ear when it's asked for, you pray. You make a few mistakes on the way. But we each play only a small part in another person's life.

Will there be someone there at the next stage? Will Mutiara follow up those contacts? She might, if she's lonely. And she *will* be lonely, at first. Bewildered, I should think — one lame ant in that teaming, thrusting ant-hill of a city. I'm sure the Lord is at work in her life — but she's wriggling, isn't she? I hope she finds good friends who'll care for her, show her God's love. I hope David will write to her; and Ani. Students sometimes mean to write, and then don't. And what about the missionaries? Will they write too, and pray for her? Or will they push her, in their busyness, to the back of their minds; one among many? Will their prayer-partners remember Mutiara? There may not be much news to send them.

Mutiara is a fictional character, and so are David and the rest. But their experiences are very similar to those of many young people here in North Sumatra. We ourselves, or our fellow missionaries, would be happy to tell you more about these real people. Some are your brothers and sisters (if you are a Christian), and others we hope one day will be too — in God's grace and through all our prayers.

In Christ's fellowship,
Anne Ruck.

Did you enjoy reading this book? If so, here are some more you might like.

GOD WAS A STRANGER
Set in a crisis period of modern Indonesian history, this book tells the story of Chepto, a teenage boy searching for something worthwhile to do with his life. Through his personal frustrations and conflicts and those of his country, Chepto finds the answer in the God who is no longer a stranger.

TO A DIFFERENT DRUM
"Grabbing my sickle from the table, Mike began to run, heading for the gate. As soon as I realized what was happening I tore right after him — I wasn't going to have him kill his father with my sickle!"

What had brought Pauline Hamilton, a physiology Ph.D, to work with delinquent boys in Taiwan? Why had she chosen to march to a different drum from her contemporaries?

IN HIS TIME
Ian Gordon-Smith was killed in a road accident in Thailand, along with eleven other missionaries and children. Assured of a brilliant future, he had been willing to sacrifice it in order to be obedient to the Lord he loved. This moving story is told by his mother mainly through his diaries.

WHEN GOD GUIDES
Does God guide individuals? Is guidance confined to the big things of life, or can I refer everything to Him? In this book guidance is clothed in flesh and blood, as 27 people share their experiences in relation to marriage and children, houses and staff, missionary call and type of work, and the manifold details of everyday life.